The Ultimate Guide to
Unarmed Self Defense

David J. Erath Jr.

The Ultimate Guide to Unarmed Self Defense
by David J. Erath Jr.

Published by David J. Erath Jr.
contact@functionalselfdefense.org
http://www.functionalselfdefense.org

Note to the reader:

The information presented in this book can be dangerous, and can result in serious injury or death. It is provided for information purposes only. Anyone practicing any technique in this book does so at their own risk. Furthermore, before starting any physical training, a physician should be consulted first.

It is the reader's responsibility to comply with self defense law and justified use of force. The author, publisher, and distributor of this book assume no responsibility for the use or misuse of the information contained within.

Table of Contents

Acknowledgments.. vi

Forward.. vii

Chapter 1: Self Defense vs. Martial Arts............................. 1
1.2 Legal Ramifications.. 3
1.3 What Is FSD... 3
1.4 Why Techniques Are Not Enough................................... 5

Chapter 2: The Truth About Violence.................................. 8
2.1 The Nature Of Physical Violence................................... 8
2.2 Martial Arts Myths... 9
2.3 Acting Tough Is For Losers.. 9

Chapter 3: Avoidance, Awareness, & Prevention................ 11
3.1 The Short Version... 12
3.2 The Detailed Version.. 12
3.2.1 Avoid Dangerous Places... 13
3.2.2 Be a Bad Target.. 14
3.2.2 Obstacles And Home Security..................................... 15
3.2.3 Be Aware Of Your Surroundings................................ 17
3.2.3 Warning Signs.. 18
3.2.3 Pre-Attack Indicators... 18
3.2.4 How To Prevent The Attack.. 21
3.2.5 Distance Is Prevention.. 22
3.2.6 Evasion... 22
3.2.7 De-escalation.. 23
3.2.7 Verbal Compliance... 23
3.2.7 Verbal And Physical Dominance................................ 24
3.2.7 Physical Compliance.. 24
3.3 The OODA Loop... 26
3.4 Preventing The Freeze.. 28
3.5 Violence, Danger, And Paranoia.................................... 29

Chapter 4: The Covered Blast... 29
4.1 Why Cover Is Crucial... 32
4.2 What Exactly Is Cover?.. 34
4.3 Examples.. 37

Chapter 5: Functional Self Defense Training 43

5.1 Training Methods And Issues 45
5.1.1 Solo Training 39
5.1.2 Cooperative Partner Training 40
5.1.3 Sparring 48
5.1.4 Random Flowing 43
5.1.5 The Greater Whole 49
5.2 The "I" Method 50
5.3 The MMA Base 52
5.4 Self Defense: Beyond The MMA Base 53
5.4.1 Self Defense Techniques 53
5.4.2 Natural Environments 53
5.4.3 Adrenal Issues 54
5.4.5 Meditation 55
5.4.6 Multiple Opponents 55
5.4.7 Weapons 56
5.5 Conditioned And Default Responses 57
5.6 Increasing Skills And Qualities 59
5.6.1 Speed 59
5.6.2 Timing 60
5.6.3 Distance And Position 62
5.6.4 Power 64
5.6.5 Accuracy 66

Chapter 6: The MMA Base 69

6.1 Footwork 71
6.1.1 Cross Footwork 71
6.1.2 Triangular Footwork 74
6.1.3 Pendulum Step 77
6.2 Boxing 79
6.2.1 The Jab 79
6.2.2 The Cross 82
6.2.3 The Hook 84
6.2.4 The Uppercut 86
6.2.5 The Catch 88
6.2.6 The Parry 90
6.2.7 The Shoulder Roll 91
6.2.8 Covers 92
6.2.9 Ducking 94
6.2.10 Bob And Weave 95
6.2.11 The Boxing Blast 97
6.3 Kick Boxing 101
6.3.1 The Groin Kick 101
6.3.2 The Side Kick 105
6.3.3 The Thai Kick 108
6.3.4 Other Kicks 110
6.3.5 Blocking Kicks 111
6.4 Knees And Elbows 114

6.4.1 Knees.. 115
6.4.2 Elbows... 120
6.5 Clinch... 124
6.5.1 The Low Tie Up... 124
6.5.1 Swimming And the Body Lock... 125
6.5.1 The Arm Drag... 127
6.5.1 The Single Underhook... 131
6.5.1 Single And Double Leg Takedowns... 133
6.5.1 Striking In The Low Tie Up... 135
6.5.2 The High Tie Up.. 137
6.6 Ground Fighting... 144
6.7 Sparring In The MMA Base.. 145
6.7.1 Sparring Variations.. 145
6.7.2 Sparring Tips... 146

Chapter 7: Functional Self Defense.. 149
7.1 FSD Control Positions.. 151
7.1.1 Head And Arm Control.. 154
7.1.1 Head And Arm Control: Striking Follow Ups..................................... 157
7.1.1 Head And Arm Control: The Duck Under... 158
7.1.1 Head And Arm Control: Kimura... 160
7.1.1 Head And Arm Control: Slings and Throws....................................... 162
7.1.1 Head And Arm Control: Holds... 165
7.1.2 Arm Control... 167
7.1.2 Arm Control: Knees And Elbows... 168
7.1.2 Arm Control: Face Grabs And Head Manipulations........................... 169
7.2 FSD Fundamental Five... 171
7.2.1 Hit And Run... 172
7.2.1 Eye Strike.. 173
7.2.1 Groin Slap.. 176
7.2.1 The Side Kick... 179
7.2.2 The Blast.. 180
7.2.2 Smack And Hack Entry.. 181
7.2.2 Palm Blast Entry.. 185
7.2.3 The Crash.. 195
7.2.4 The Crack.. 200
7.2.5 Takedown Defense... 203
7.2.6 Clinch Entry.. 206

Chapter 8: Environmental Applications................................. 209
8.1 Pre-Positioning.. 212
8.2 Using Your Environment.. 218

Chapter 9: Physical and Mental Fitness................................ 219
9.1 Exercise.. 221
9.2 Diet.. 222
9.3 Meditation.. 222

Chapter 10: Frequently Asked Questions..225

What should I do if I don't have a training partner?...226

How can I train alone?..226

What is the best self defense I can learn if I don't have much time for training?..............227

What is the best self defense for women?...227

I have young children. What is the best self defense for them?..........................228

How long will it take me to learn self defense?..228

What is the best self defense to avoid injuring my opponent?............................229

How can I defend against a bigger/faster/stronger opponent?............................229

What can I do to improve my footwork?...230

What do you think about (insert specific martial art)?..231

What are your thoughts on Krav Maga?...232

Can you recommend a martial art for me to take?...232

What can I do to become more comfortable sparring or fighting?......................233

How safe is getting punched in the head during training?..................................233

Do you recommend carrying a weapon? And if so, what weapon?.....................234

What is chi power, and how can I learn to use it?..235

What do you think about using pressure points for self defense?.......................236

You claim that (insert martial art) isn't effective? How can that be so?.............236

Acknowledgments

This book would not have been possible without support from a great variety of people.

From the beginning, my parents, David and Carol Erath, taught me that it was ok to question everything and to make my own way. Keeping an open but sceptical mind and not giving undue respect to authority kept me from getting stuck in any particular style or path, and without that, FSD and this book would not have been possible.

Although I moved on to entirely different systems, my first teachers and practice partners were instrumental in my development, and an inspiration to me. Elmer Glover Jr., Darrin Duroncelet, and Matt Foss, to this day, are still the most powerful and fastest people I have ever learned from or trained with. They gave me more bruises, lumps, and sprains in 5 years than I've gotten since. Everything I do now is still informed by the skills and qualities I learned from them.

My first small but serious group of students and training partners - Taylor Clark, Joey Cook, my cousins Daniel and Jeff Erath, my uncle Harold Erath, Lacey Lee, William May, and my sister Becky Orozco - put up with a lot, from injuries to constantly changing material. During my most experimental time, I couldn't have done it without their support. A number of my long term private students, who stuck with me through still more changes, provided both necessary physical and financial support. Ada Carrik, Pat Flower, Tony Hart, Jason Hadley, Bill Hall, Eric Hussey, Julie Jones, Andre Laborde, Al Palumbo, David Parsiola, Trina Shoemaker, Dean Taylor, Nigel Thibodeaux, Jimmie Washburn, and Jason Witham.

I've had many martial arts teachers along the way, the lesser known of which have often given me the most. Danny Terrell not only put up with my questioning, but also encouraged it, and taught me a lot. Sydney Zaffuto, who made the right choice but was murdered despite it, also taught me a great deal in our relatively short time together. Rory Miller's work on violence and prevention caused me to more seriously and systematically incorporate that vital element of self defense into my teaching. Maija Soderholm's work has also had a substantial influence on my practice and teaching. And Matt Thornton's work, particularly on "aliveness" and the "I Method", has informed my practice for many years.

Dragan Aleksic, my friend and training partner for the last couple of years, has been a great and valuable help. James Wilson, another friend and training partner in the Filipino martial arts, has made significant contributions to my material. Mario Igrec has given me important technical support and encouragement in writing this book. And, Daniel Erath, my cousin, friend, and primary training partner for nearly 20 years, featured with me in the pictures in this book...has helped me more than I can say.

Finally, and most importantly, my wife, photographer, and editor, Birgit Erath. Despite being a penniless martial arts instructor when we first met, she believed in me, married me, and stuck with me through years of difficult financial times. She never for a moment questioned or doubted my choices, and has always given me support in every way. I have benefited immeasurably from her help, creativity, scepticism, and curiosity.

So to all of you, and anyone I may have unfortunately forgot, thank you!

Forward

This book is the condensed result of more than 20 years of learning, practice, and teaching. It covers unarmed self defense, that is, defense against unarmed attacks without the use of weapons. However, the material on violence, awareness, and prevention applies to both unarmed and armed attacks.

I have tried to make this book as comprehensive as possible, and the progression is the same as I would use in teaching. My goal is for a person with this book, a training partner or two, time, and dedication, to be able to learn to defend themselves against unarmed attacks, without using a weapon. (My next book will cover defense against weapons and using weapons in self defense.) Training with a good, qualified instructor and a group of students with a variety of body types would be ideal. But unfortunately there are very few functional self defense schools. Most schools today either focus on a single, limited martial art with limited functional application, or sport based systems that lack many components necessary for use in self defense. Therefore, this book can function as a stand alone source for people with no access to quality self defense instruction, or as a compliment and/or addition to good instruction and training.

Although material throughout this book can be taken in isolated parts, the progression of all of the material is important. A practitioner should begin by understanding the nature of self defense (Chapter 1), and violence, awareness, and prevention (Chapters 2 and 3). Without understanding the "what", the "how" makes little sense. Chapter 4 details the concept of the *Covered Blast*, which should inform the practice and training of everything that follows. Chapter 5 covers functional training, and is absolutely essential. Without functional training, the techniques in the rest of this book will be useless, and many people wrongly assume that their training is functional when it is not. Chapter 6, on the *MMA Base*, will give a practitioner the foundation they need to execute the more effective techniques in Chapter 7, under extreme aggressive pressure. I chose to present "control positions" first in Chapter 7, along with follow ups, as the control positions and their follow ups are the key to reliably taking out an opponent. It would be a mistake to practice the techniques in Chapter 7 without understanding how they relate to the control positions and follow ups. Chapter 8 deals with the application of physical self defense in natural environments. Chapter 9 covers physical and mental fitness, which are very important, if not essential. And Chapter 10 answers many common questions not already specifically covered.

I have spent well over a year writing this book, going over every word, and often re-writing sections or even entire chapters to be as clear as possible. There is more to it than one might discover in a single reading. And many if not all of the techniques will take years to fully learn and appreciate. My goal in my own practice and teaching has always been to find the most efficient and effective solutions for self defense. The techniques detailed in this book have been chosen with careful consideration, based on decades of practice and application with a great variety of people. They work. And they work extremely well. I am confident that if a practitioner trains the techniques using functional training methods, they will also find them to be exceptionally efficient and effective.

In addition to this book, my website, http://www.functionalselfdefense.org, has a great deal of free information, pictures, and videos. If you subscribe to my website and blog, you'll not only find more techniques and training tips, but also notifications when I release new books or videos. If you have any questions or comments, please feel free to contact me at contact@functionalselfdefense.org.

Chapter 1
Self Defense vs. Martial Arts

1.1 Self Defense vs. Martial Arts

Most martial arts have roots in armed combat and war, many dating back before the use of guns. The goal of these original martial arts was to incapacitate an opponent through injury or death. Self defense is much more than that. While self defense may require a practitioner to injure or kill an opponent with techniques that can be found in martial arts, the goal of self defense is your own survival and prosperity.

There is an important distinction to be made between taking out an opponent and avoiding injury or death for yourself and those you care about. Taking out an opponent may be necessary, but more often than not, it isn't. Knowing when to fight and when not to fight can make the difference between permanent injury or disability even if you do "win", suffering retaliation or having to hide for the rest of your life, going to jail, or getting sued in the aftermath. In self defense, the goal is far more desirable than in martial arts. Survival and prosperity always beat taking an opponent out.

Over time, many well known traditional martial arts have developed peaceful philosophies or entirely new purposes as the countries from which they came became more and more peaceful. In Japan for example, the killing art of *kenjutsu* was transformed into the sport of *kendo*. *Ju jutsu* changed to *judo*. And *karate-jutsu* changed to *karate-do*. Similar transformations have occurred in martial arts around the world. But the change from martial arts to martial sports or martial ways (*bujutsu,* with an emphasis on damaging techniques, to *budo,* with an emphasis on discipline and morals) has not made these systems any more effective for self defense. In fact, the opposite is generally true. As martial arts have become martial sports and ways, and correspondingly less damaging, they've moved further away from self defense. While many styles do have peaceful philosophies, they've simply dropped their formerly aggressive nature. Practitioners no longer understand the nature of physical violence, and these systems have not added components to teach awareness and prevention. They've lost their combative edge without adding anything to compensate.

The majority of martial arts are limited in terms of style. Some only teach striking, some only grappling, some only with weapons, and some only unarmed. There are martial arts that specialize in linear movements and footwork, and others that specialize in circular movements. Functional self defense includes it all. There is no style in self defense, only what works. A self defense practitioner must not only understand violence, awareness, and prevention, but also how to fight standing, in a clinch, on the ground, and with and against weapons. Functional self defense is comprehensive. Martial arts are nearly always limited.

1.2 Legal Ramifications

Understanding when you can use physical self defense is extraordinarily important. Going to jail and/ or getting sued can destroy your life, not to mention the lives of your family members. If you're going to practice physical self defense, you need to know when you can use it and when you cannot. In most countries and jurisdictions, legal self defense can only be established if:

- You are free from fault or provocation.
- You have no means of escape or retreat.
- You or another person are in immediate danger of physical harm.

In addition, in many jurisdictions *you can only use the minimum level of force required to remove the threat.* If you engaged in an argument before the fight, it may not be legally justifiable. If you could have escaped but didn't, it may not be legally justifiable. If you were not in immediate danger of physical harm, or another reasonable person would not have felt such danger, it may not be legally justifiable. And if you continue to attack after the threat is removed, it may not be legally justifiable.

Physical self defense must only be used as an absolute last resort, and you should be able to communicate your compliance with the above conditions to law enforcement officials. Otherwise, you risk going to prison and being sued. **Take this seriously!**

1.3 What Is FSD?

FSD (Functional Self Defense) is a comprehensive combination of strategies, training methods, and techniques designed to provide practitioners with highly efficient and effective self defense skills. It covers all ranges (stand up, clinch, and ground) and areas of self defense, from awareness and nonphysical prevention to the use of weapons and multiple opponents.

Guiding Principles and Concepts

Self Defense Emphasis: FSD is first and foremost a self defense system. In that regard, function is always more important than form, and all techniques, training methods, and strategies are evaluated based on applications to functional self defense.

Progressive Resistance: Training is done with progressive resistance, such that during the introductory phase of a technique or training method the intensity level is low, but gradually progresses higher and higher as the practitioner's skill level increases. A real attacker will not attack slowly and easily, so in order to learn to defend against a real attack, every practitioner must train techniques against high intensity attacks and with high intensity resistance.

With that said, all training should not be at 100% intensity, as training at such a level increases the risk of injury. Most training can take place at moderate intensity, but every practitioner should have some experience with 100% intensity and resistance.

Uncooperative Partners: All techniques must be trained and applied against completely uncooperative partners. Keep in mind that resistance does not equal entirely uncooperative. There is a difference, and resistance is not enough. Training must be done against a partner who is completely uncooperative in every way, trying his best not to let the practitioner accomplish his goals. However, all training should not be completely uncooperative. In some training methods practitioners will be cooperative. In others (boxing style sparring, wrestling, etc.), practitioners will be somewhat uncooperative with limitations. But because a real attacker will be uncooperative and unpredictable, every practitioner should train at various levels of intensity against a completely uncooperative opponent.

Footwork/Movement: Footwork and/or movement should be a part of every technique or drill. In real attacks, people move, a lot. No one stands still when they're struck. They either move when they're struck, or they move in order to get out of the way of the strike. Combination attacks must be trained with footwork/movement, as no opponent will be in the same place after the initial attack is launched. Movement with defensive techniques is equally important. Standing in place while attempting to defend allows the attacker to continuously attack.

All Offense: Defense isn't what puts an opponent out of commission. Offense is. Every defense should be offensive in one way or another, either as a damaging attack or to gain positive position/control, or combined with a simultaneous offensive action. Blocking first and countering second, as is common in a great many martial arts, is a recipe for failure. Only in movies and cooperative training does one person attack, have the attack blocked, and wait for his opponent to have his turn. When a person attempts to block first and counter second, the attacker will most likely continue his attack, never allowing an opportunity for a one-then-two counter. Instead, strive to attack before or during/into the attack. Attack on the opponent's preparation, on his motion of convergence, or simultaneously. It may be the case that a purely defensive move is inadvertently made against a surprise attack, however the ability to counter into a continuing attack, rather than waiting for the opponent to stop, is essential.

Covered Blast: Use a combination of distance, position, and offensive and defensive techniques to minimize the opponent's options while maximizing your own. See Chapter 4 for detailed information on the Covered Blast.

Openness: Maintain an open, inquisitive, and sceptical mind with regard to *everything*. We are products of our experiences, and those experiences are both specific and limited. To maximize our knowledge and skills, we must be willing and able to learn from new information, especially when it conflicts with our current thinking. In order to maintain an open mind, we cannot hold anything or anyone as sacred, always right, or above questioning. There is *nothing* we truly know, 100%. No one does.

1.4 Why Techniques Are Not Enough

Techniques are the most easily identifiable part of any self defense system or martial art. Some schools focus almost exclusively on techniques, as do many books and videos. But techniques are perhaps the least important of the three fundamental components of physical self defense: *techniques*, *training methods*, and *strategy*.

Techniques alone are useless. They require training methods that give the practitioner the skills to apply them under pressure, with the speed, power, leverage, timing, and flexibility necessary to make them work. And even with good training methods, without strategy, a practitioner won't know when to apply techniques.

Techniques do not exist in isolation. They must be applied against a violent, fully resisting, uncooperative opponent. There will be movement, speed, changes in direction, and an overall state of chaos. This is the environment in which self defense techniques are applied. Therefore, they must be supported by training methods that mirror that environment, or increase the skills necessary to apply them there.

In the first martial arts books I ever bought, on Japanese ju jutsu, techniques were referred to as "tricks". There were finger locking tricks, wrist locking tricks, throwing tricks, etc. Each technique was demonstrated on a man who was standing still and fully cooperating. There was no discussion whatsoever of training or strategy. While learning the mechanics of a technique on a cooperative opponent is necessary, that cannot be the extent of training.

In addition to training being required to support techniques, it takes strategy to know when to apply a technique, which technique to apply, and how to apply it. Should you attack first, or intercept? Strike, or grapple? Should you use a weapon? Should you enter straight in, or at an angle? Which techniques will you use against various types of opponents and in various situations? Will you do the same thing if you're attacked by one person, alone, or if you're attacked with a family member? What if you're attacked by multiple opponents? Is there a difference between how you'll act if you're attacked on the street vs. inside your home? These questions, and many more, are highly important, and all under the domain of strategy.

With excellent strategy and training, even poor techniques can be made to work against an average opponent. But without strategy and training, even excellent techniques will fail against the most unskilled opponent.

Take-Aways

- Self defense is comprehensive, whereas martial arts are limited.
- Physical self defense must be legally justifiable.
- Progressive resistance and uncooperative partners are essential.
- Footwork/movement should be a part of every technique and training method.
- Offense beats defense.
- Techniques are not enough. Realistic training and strategy is also a necessity.
- Maintain an open, inquisitive, and sceptical mind.

Chapter 2
The Truth About Violence

The Truth About Violence

For the vast majority of people reading this, *violence is **easy** to prevent without resorting to physical self defense*. Additionally, non-physical means have a far lower level of risk and higher chance of success. It may not seem that way, especially to those who have fallen victim to misleading martial arts and self defense marketing, but I hope the next chapter, which covers avoidance, awareness, and prevention, will make that clear. *Most people do not need to learn martial arts in order to prevent being attacked.* There are many misconceptions about violence, and the purpose of this chapter is to help shed light on the nature of serious violence and common problems in physical self defense and martial arts training. If you follow the information and advice in the following chapter on prevention, the material in this chapter should be largely unnecessary. But if you don't follow that advice, if you find yourself in an unavoidable physical conflict, or if you're simply interested in being able to physically defend yourself even if the chance you'll need to is low, the following material will be valuable.

2.1 The Nature of Physical Violence

Real violence is fast, dynamic, and chaotic. At least one person in the encounter will be trying to injure another, and neither person will know what the other will do next. It's not what you see in most movies or learn about in most martial arts classes. The images above are from a real assault, captured by a security camera I had installed outside an old house of mine. The woman was walking along the sidewalk when a truck stopped, a man got out, and ran at her. She froze for a moment in fear, and was tackled in a bear hug onto my concrete steps. As soon as she hit the steps the man was yelling and cursing at her, choking her, and slamming her head into the steps. He then dragged her into his truck and drove away.

The bear hug wasn't at all like bear hugs trained in most martial arts or self defense classes. It lasted about one second, and was only used to slam the woman. The choke wasn't standing, and it wasn't on a flat surface where common counters are trained. Not only was the woman on an uneven surface, but she was getting her head repeatedly slammed into the steps and screamed at while being choked. This is what a real assault is like.

In any attack where you can legally defend yourself, your opponent(s) will probably have a significant advantage over you, or at the very least a perceived advantage. There will be more than one, they'll have weapons, and/or they'll be bigger, stronger, and faster than you. If they don't think they have an advantage, they'll choose another victim. Real violence is ugly, and it is best avoided or prevented.

2.2 Martial Arts Myths

The vast majority of martial arts today do not prepare practitioners for real assaults. They don't address avoidance, awareness, and prevention, don't have effective strategies for dealing with an assault or training methods that work, the techniques are designed for art or sport rather than for doing maximum damage, and they fail to address weapon use and defense and multiple opponents. All training takes place in well lit rooms, on clean, flat surfaces with nothing to trip over or run into, and in clothing that's easiest for moving around in. Mock attacks are generally done with "proper form". They're single attacks or easy to identify techniques one after another, and the "bad guy" doesn't fight back after his initial attack is blocked.

Real attacks occur in real places, not empty training rooms. Outdoors there are curbs to trip over, cars and steps to fall on, walls and corners to get rammed into, and good places for an attacker to hide in order to rush out and surprise you. Indoors there is limited space to move around, with plenty furniture to fall over or get knocked or slammed into. There are objects all over that can be used to beat or stab you. Your attacker(s) will likely have a weapon anyway. It's likely to be dark, and you won't be able to see well. You may not even know if your attacker has a weapon or not, even after you've been stabbed, slashed, or beaten with it. Real assaults generally involve a great deal of movement and chaos. They are nothing like what most martial artists train for.

Martial sports (boxing, Thai boxing, judo, and Brazilian jiu jitsu for example) do a good job of preparing students to deal with an entirely uncooperative opponent. However, they focus on one-on-one "fights", with limited techniques and ranges, between two willing participants, without weapons, and in clean spaces designed for fighting. Many traditional martial arts claim to focus more on self defense, but fail to train against uncooperative opponents who are fighting back. In reality, although they may use more potentially dangerous techniques in training, students of these styles are even less prepared to deal with a real attack than those who train in martial sports, due to their lack of familiarity with noncooperative environments. The coming chapter on training will cover this in detail, along with all of the concepts and drills necessary to create physical self defense ability.

2.3 Acting Tough Is For Losers

Accurately writing about violence is a challenge. One one hand, it's important to explain the nature of violence and the problems with most martial arts and self defense training. On the other hand, scary and tough talk can be damaging and counterproductive. Violence is negative and destructive, and becoming paranoid or obsessing about crime will decrease your quality of life. You can avoid or prevent an attack or physically defend yourself without becoming obsessed with violence, wearing camouflage pants, and carrying three knives to the bathroom.

It's easy for people to take self defense too far, to let it change their lives for the worse. Negative thoughts, words, and actions produce negative feelings and make the world a worse place for us all. Positive thoughts, words, and actions do the opposite. They make the world a better place for us all.

Although violence is ugly, it's unnecessary to act tough or imagine you're a pseudo-special forces operative in order to defend yourself. In fact, such behavior will likely make you a more attractive target for people looking to start trouble.

There are two very different approaches you can take to self defense. You can act with the intention of defending yourself, or you can act with the intention of hurting another person. Both approaches can work for self defense. But the first will make you a happier, more likeable person. The second will make you a negative, fearful, and paranoid person. Acting tough is for losers.

Take-Aways

- Violence is easy to prevent without physical self defense.
- Real physical violence is fast, dynamic, and chaotic.
- Assaults take place in "messy" environments, very different from typical training rooms.
- Training must mirror reality in order to work in reality.
- You don't need to obsess about violence or become a "tough guy" to be able to deal with it.

Chapter 3
Awareness, Avoidance, & Prevention

Avoidance, Awareness, & Prevention

3.1 The Short Version:

Avoiding or preventing an attack is easy, and in the vast majority of situations it does not require physical self defense or martial arts. If you follow these simple guidelines, the chance you'll ever be attacked is incredibly small:

- Avoid dangerous places and people.
- Don't be a good target.
- Be aware of your surroundings.
- Do not argue, provoke, or allow a verbal conflict to escalate.
- Escape or create distance if you feel threatened.
- Give up your money or valuables if bodily harm is threatened and you cannot escape.
- Keep your private areas secure.

What are dangerous places? How can you avoid being a good target? How and when should you attempt to escape? Read on.

3.2 The Detailed Version:

For a predator to attack you, he necessarily needs three things: *intent, means,* and *opportunity*. Denying him any one of those three things makes it impossible for him to attack. The easiest way to do that is to avoid a predator so completely that he is not only denied the *opportunity* to attack you, but also the *intent* as it specifically relates to you. If you're not on his radar, he can't even intend to attack you. You can accomplish this to a very significant degree simply by avoiding dangerous places. If you're unable to avoid a predator, making yourself a bad target is the next best thing.

If a predator does choose you as a target, you can still deny him the *opportunity* to attack you. By being aware of your surroundings, paying attention to warning signs, and noticing pre-attack indicators, you can spot a predator and deny him the close distance he needs to attack you by using space and/or objects in your environment. And even if you are approached by a predator, you can de-escalate the situation and avoid physical violence using a variety of measures.

If you've taken the steps above, it's highly unlikely it will go that far. But even when a predator has the *intent* and *opportunity* to attack, we can take away his *means* or ability through physical self defense.

In the rest of this chapter, I'll cover avoiding dangerous places, being a bad target, being aware of your surroundings, warning signs, pre-attack indicators, distance, evasion, de-escalation, pre-positioning, and physical self defense strategy. In the rest of this book, I'll cover taking away a predator's means through physical self defense.

3.2.1 Avoid Dangerous Places

This is the number one rule of self defense. If you avoid places where violence is likely to occur, you'll dramatically decrease the chance you'll even be considered as a target. These are dangerous places:

High Crime Areas: Some countries, cities, and areas are known for having high levels of crime. Even in regions that are generally safe, there are often specific geographic locations where high levels of crime regularly occur. Even if violence in such areas isn't targeting people like you, it's possible to get caught in the crossfire. In your own city, if there are high crime areas, you probably know where they are. Avoid them. Don't travel to other cities or countries with high crime rates. If you do enjoy travelling, there is a lifetime of safe destinations to visit. Travelling to a dangerous city or country is not worth the risk, particularly when there are so many safe alternatives. Before travelling to a new destination, look into the crime statistics and avoid the high crime areas.

Among Violent People: Violence is more likely to occur in the presence of violent people. Obviously the former section, *high crime areas*, ranks at the top of the list for being *among violent people*. In addition, violence often takes place where groups of young males hang out, particularly where they're drinking. If you avoid bars, parties, and other such locations, the chance you'll even see such violence is slim. If you're not a young male, then these locations won't pose the same level of risk. Violence is also common in violent groups, but exposure to it requires being in a group with a propensity toward violence. If you're not a member of a violent group, you don't hang out in the same places as such groups, and you're not in a relationship with a violent individual, you're covered. If you are a member of a violent group, or you're in a relationship with a violent individual, there's only one thing you need to do: *Get out now*. It may not be easy, but you can do it.

Among People Who Don't Like You: Places where you're different from everyone else *and* where that difference isn't well accepted can be dangerous. If you're a white American male walking around in Tokyo, it's highly unlikely you're going to have a problem, even though you are different and you will stick out. But if you're a white American male walking around in Afghanistan...well that's a different story. Avoid places where you'll stick out *and* people tend not to like your kind.

Verbal Escalations: When two or more people begin to argue, with escalating verbal tension, the likelihood of violence increases. Some individuals need to psych themselves up in order to become violent, and progress from talking quietly and being relatively still to yelling and using bigger physical movements before becoming physically violent. Verbal conflicts can happen in any physical location, but because they require an escalation, you can avoid that "place". *Avoid arguments, conflicts, and provoking people*. And remember, it's possible for a person to perceive that you provoked them even if you think otherwise. It's better to be even nicer and less provocative than you may think necessary. Tread carefully in places or groups where you don't know the social conventions.

In-Between Places: Violence is easier to successfully use and get away with where there are few witnesses. But there must be someone available to attack. "In-between places" are those where people commonly pass through, but not *too* frequently, for example, between parking lots and tourist attractions, on jogging and hiking trails, on isolated side streets, in parking garages, and on the way to mail rooms from apartment complexes. Attackers can wait in these places, knowing that victims will pass through, and they'll likely have some time alone with the victim. In-between places where people are more likely to have money or valuables are an even better location for criminals looking for money.

As best you can, avoid these in-between-places. If you're staying in a hotel that's several blocks away from tourist attractions, and getting to the attraction requires a walk down an isolated street, take a cab instead of walking. If you're going to a popular area but know you won't be able to find parking in the vicinity, take a cab or public transportation if it exists. If you're going to a shopping mall and have the choice to park in an isolated parking garage or a visible lot on the street, choose the visible lot on the street. *Imagine you need to rob someone for money, tonight. Think about where you would wait for victims, and avoid those places.*

A rapist or serial killer doesn't need his victim to have money, and may be willing to wait for a longer period of time. If you were a rapist and wanted to ambush a woman, where would you do it? On a jogging trail near a college campus, but not *too* near? On a path between an apartment complex and the mail room, not visible from the street? Avoid these in-between-places if possible, and when you can't, be sure to follow the rest of the advice in this chapter.

Lawless Places: Some countries and areas are relatively lawless, particularly in times of war and internal conflict. In these places, criminals can get away with nearly anything. Avoid these places. If you chose not to avoid them, then minimize your time and exposure in them.

3.2.2 Be A Bad Target

Often times a predator will choose his targets based on some conception of risk vs. reward. The predator wants to get one or more things out of the attack (reward), and minimize his chance of getting injured or caught in the process (risk). There are exceptions, as some predators may be reckless, mentally ill, without self-worth, suicidal, or under the influence of drugs. But consider that very few robbers will attempt to rob a policeman in uniform, but many will rob a well dressed woman with an expensive purse, lots of jewelry, and headphones in her ears. Anything you can do to increase the risk and decrease the rewards for a potential predator, will decrease the chance that you'll be chosen as a target.

Increasing Risks

In general, a predator will choose victims they think they can successfully attack. While you can't change your age, height, and gender, there are some things you can do to make yourself a higher risk target. Paying attention to your surroundings is a big one, which I'll cover in more detail shortly, but if a predator sees he'll be unable to take you by surprise, he'll probably choose a target who is paying less attention. Walking around with headphones in your ears, listening to music, talking on the phone, or texting, is a sure sign you're not paying attention. Avoid these behaviors, *especially* in isolated areas. Along similar lines, don't get drunk in public. Drunk people make perfect victims.

When people are physically fit, it shows. And attacking a fit person is more risky than attacking one who is visibly out of shape. Aside from the mental and physical benefits, regular exercise and weight lifting will make you a higher risk target.

The clothing a person is wearing can inhibit movement. Who would you prefer to attack, a woman in a tight skirt with high heal shoes, or a woman wearing jeans and running shoes? The clothing and shoes a person wears can tell a predator a lot about them. Wear clothing that allows you to move well.

One person is easier to attack than two, two people are easier to attack than three, and so on. While groups can get attacked, the more people you're with, the lower your chances will be.

If you know how to use it, carrying a visible weapon can significantly increase the risk to a potential attacker. Would you rather attack a woman with pepper spray in her hand, or one with nothing? Think about the type of person you'd choose to attack if you needed to get money today, if you were a rapist, or if you wanted to beat someone up to prove your manhood. What behaviors, qualities, and conditions would make you more likely to attack them? What behaviors, qualities, and conditions would make you less likely to attack them?

Decreasing Rewards

Again, you can't change certain aspects of your physicality. But you can change aspects of your behavior that would be rewarding to a predator. What does wearing expensive clothing and jewellery tell a predator looking for money? What kind of car do you drive, and what does it tell a potential predator? What does wearing revealing clothing show a man who is already thinking about rape? (It's not fair, but it is true.) Think about what you'd look for in a victim, in terms of rewards, and eliminate those as best you can. When a woman carries a purse, it wouldn't be foolish to assume there are objects in it, potentially valuable objects, especially if it's an expensive, name-brand purse. If you do need to pass through a high risk area, don't carry or wear anything that will appeal to a predator. This includes laptops, smart phones, and any other high value items you may carry in your hand or wear on your body.

Obstacles & Home Security

The more obstacles a potential predator has to deal with, the more likely he'll choose an easier target. Would you prefer to break into a home with a visible camera, motion sensing lights, window bars, a barking dog, and an obvious alarm system, or one with no sign of preventative obstacles? In addition to the deterrent quality of obstacles, some can stop an attacker dead in his tracks. If you do have an alarm system, *use it*!

Keep your home, car doors, and windows locked. Don't open the door for strangers. A locked door is an obstacle that requires far more effort to get through than one that is unlocked. And when that locked door has a sign next to it from an alarm company, and a dog barking behind it, there are very few predators that won't leave for another home.

Some predators will walk a neighborhood pretending to be a handyman, knocking on doors to see who is home, who isn't, who opens doors, and what's inside. Again, do not open the door for strangers. Use blinds or curtains so it's difficult for a predator to easily see inside your house. Use motion activated lights around your house. Predators don't want to be seen, and will avoid getting close to a motion acti-vated light. The more obstacles you can set up between you and an attacker, the harder it will be for him to reach you, and the more likely it will be that he'll chose another victim.

Have a plan for home invasions, and make sure everyone in your home knows that plan. Your plan will vary depending on the size and layout of your home, where the exits are, how many people live in it, their ages, etc. When making your plan, remember that the goal isn't to kill an intruder, but to keep yourself and your family safe. Escaping may be your first priority, particularly if you know where the intrud-ers are coming in, have barriers between them and your family, and a safe way to exit. If you do have motion sensing lights, locked doors and windows, an alarm system, and an alert dog, it's highly unlikely your home will be chosen. If it is, each of these barriers will act as layers in your security system, alert-ing you to the progress of the intruders.

Some people have a philosophical problem with owning or using guns. Although I'd prefer if no one was violent or used guns, that's clearly not the world we live in. I once had an instructor in a handgun course explain that a gun is like a parachute. No one wants to have to use a parachute. But if you were in a plane that was going down, and you had the opportunity to jump out with a parachute, you sure would be glad you had one. I feel the same way about guns, and it's a valid argument, regardless of how you feel about them. If intruders ignore your motion sensing lights, break through your door or window, continue into your home despite your alarm going off, and are about to enter the room you and your family are waiting in, having a gun, the ability to use it, and a plan with a good chance of success would surely beat the alternative.

The use of guns is beyond the scope of this book. But I'll relate two incidents that happened to friends of mine here, as a cautionary note.

One friend who was a cop, had a gun on the side of his car seat. He and his fiancée stopped at a drive up ATM machine to get money, when a man approached the open car window and told my friend to hand over the money he had just retrieved. My friend went for his gun, was shot in the head, and killed in front of his fiancée.

Another couple I'm friends with was asleep in their home, when my friend woke up and noticed his kitchen light on in the room next to their bedroom. He had a gun under his bed, right next to him. But before he could grab it, the door opened up and a man came in with a gun pointed at them. He was smart, and didn't go for his gun. Unfortunately their dog began barking at the guy, and the guy shot their dog in the head before robbing them. My friends left their house that night and never went back in. They put it up for sale and moved out of the city.

I relate those stories to emphasize that if you do decide to own a gun, you absolutely must learn how to use it, and you absolutely must have a plan for when to use it and when not to use it. A gun is not a magic weapon. If someone has a gun pointed at you, and you go for your gun, you're probably going to get shot. In order to use your gun, you need to know your attacker is coming BEFORE he sees you or has his gun on you. This is one reason layers of home security are so important, as they'll let you know someone is on their way.

Back to home security...

Although you won't be there to attack, if you go out of town, make sure you have a neighbor pick up your mail and remove flyers each day. Some predators will place flyers on or in front of doors, or on car windshields, to see if they get removed. If they don't get removed, they can assume you're out of town.

3.2.3 Be Aware Of Your Surroundings

It's always better to be aware and mindful, not just for self defense. Get into the habit.

Most people do the same things day after day, week after week, month after month. You should be aware of what's normal in your neighborhood, where you walk your dog, in and around public transit areas, in and around your place of work, in the grocery store parking lot, and everywhere else you go. What kind of people do you normally see? What do they normally wear? What are they normally doing?

When something or someone is out of place, take note.

Why is there an adult man hanging around a children's playground if he doesn't have a child? Why is there a man leaning against a wall or peaking out from a recessed doorway? Why did those three guys split up but keep walking toward me? Why is that man wearing a jacket in the summer? Why does that kid have one hand behind his back? I've never seen that guy before...what's he doing in my neighborhood?

People naturally have good instincts, and it's extremely common for victims of crime after the fact to say they had a bad feeling about a situation, that something or someone didn't seem right. But they ignored it. When you've got a bad feeling, *pay attention to it*!

Predators will use social conventions to their advantage. They know that it's rude to be rude, and that nice people don't want to be rude. They know you'll feel strange crossing the street when they're walking toward you, and that you probably won't. They know you probably won't tell them to get out of your face when they come too close, or that you'll shake their hand when they put it out for you. The most dangerous predators won't seem like predators on the surface, but odds are, you'll know something isn't right. They'll be where they don't belong or they'll be doing something a normal person wouldn't do. It may be something small, but if you're aware and paying attention, you'll see it. And you don't have to be paranoid. You simply need to be aware and pay attention to your feelings.

Warning Signs

Gavin de Becker, in *The Gift of Fear* covers 7 tactics a predator will commonly use to gain your trust or take advantage of you. I won't go into great detail, as you should read the book yourself, but they are worth mentioning here:

- **Forced Teaming**: The predator uses the word "we" to establish a relationship or show you have something in common. It's abnormal for a stranger to use the word "we" with you.

- **Charm**: Charm isn't a natural human trait, it requires an effort. If a stranger is charming, there's a reason. He wants something from you.

- **Too Many Details**: The predator knows he's lying, even if you don't. He'll often give you far too many details than a normal person would, in an attempt to make his story more believable.

- **Typecasting**: A predator will often attempt to put you in a group you don't want to be in, so you'll bend over backwards trying to prove you're not what he says you are - racist, rude, inconsiderate, etc. He'll do this to get you to do what he wants.

- **Loan Sharking**: The predator does something for you, so you feel the need to reciprocate. He may "help" you put your groceries in your car, open a door for you, etc.

- **Unsolicited Promise**: This is a big one, and is nearly always a sign of real trouble. A predator says, "I won't hurt you, I promise.", "I'm not one of those crazy people, I promise." If he's saying it, he's thinking about doing it.

- **Discounting the Word "No"**: Predators will discount when you tell them "no". When you tell them you don't need their help, they'll help you anyway. When you tell them no, they'll disregard it.

Most people will notice these tactics on some level. They'll feel uncomfortable, but they won't trust their instincts. It's important not only to be aware, but also to trust your feelings. *The Gift of Fear* is an excellent title, as fear really is a gift. It was given to us by nature to let us know when trouble is present. When you feel fear, there is likely a very good reason. Pay attention to it, and do something about it.

Pre-Attack Indicators

In addition to the above warning signs, there are a number of common pre-attack indicators you should be aware of. One of the most common is the ***witness check***. Before an attack, the perpetrator will know he's about to do something illegal. He either wants witnesses to see what he's doing, in the case of *violence for status*, or he wants to be sure there are no witnesses to see what he's doing, in most other cases. Many of them will do a *witness check* right before they launch their attack, looking around to check for witnesses, and some will continuously look for witnesses as the time of the attack gets nearer. If you have a strange feeling about someone, if they're somewhere they shouldn't be or doing something they shouldn't be doing, and they're looking around frequently, there is likely a problem. If a stranger has approached you, is within striking distance, and does a *witness check*, you're about to be attacked.

Highly skilled predators may operate in groups. Doing so will allow them to hide some pre-attack indicators, but this often creates others. In a team of two or more, the predator in front of you can avoid the *witness check* for example, by relying on his partner(s) as a look out. One may be approaching you from the front while another walks up from the rear. The man approaching from the front sees what's behind you, and the man coming from the rear can signal the one approaching from the front if the coast isn't clear, removing the need for the *witness check*. It's also possible for two or more predators to use cell phones for this purpose, as lookouts and to coordinate the timing of their movements.

But when predators operate in groups, they are often all within sight of each other. If you turn a corner and two men, one in front and one behind, begin walking toward you at the same time, it could be a pre-attack indicator. If you're in an isolated area and one man is leaning against a wall with a phone to his ear, and another is approaching you with a phone to his ear, but neither looks like they're talking, it may be a pre-attack indicator.

In addition to the *witness check*, many armed predators will do a **weapon check** at some distance from the victim, assuming they're not already holding the weapon (concealed or not). Obviously, the existence of a visible weapon in the hand of an approaching stranger is a very reliable pre-attack indicator. But if the weapon isn't already being held, the predator may "check" with his hand, touching his weapon (under his clothing or in his pocket) to make sure it's in position and ready. This quick pat or *weapon check* should be familiar to most people who carry or have carried a weapon.

The third common check is the **victim check**, where the attacker surveys the victim as he approaches, to make sure he's made the right choice and to monitor the victim for a weapon or counter attack. The average, relatively unskilled predator will be obvious with his *victim check*, looking the victim up and down nervously. A more skilled predator will tend to "zone out", so he can notice everything peripherally without being obvious. However, the average well-meaning stranger will not approach you in such a manner, so the *victim check* should trigger as a pre-attack indicator in most cases.

As always, there are exceptions. If a predator is sure about his location and victim choice, or if he has no regard for his own safety, he may not do any of the checks.

Some predators may avoid the *weapon check* by holding a weapon in concealment, in their pocket, behind their back, under their shirt, etc. Pay attention to where a person's hands are. If one hand is swinging naturally and another appears to be unnaturally placed in concealment, for example, this may be a pre-attack indicator.

Location can also be a pre-attack indicator. Watch for people standing or waiting where they don't belong, especially in isolated areas. Another key can be in dress. If a person is in a location they don't fit in, and they're wearing something that also doesn't fit, pay attention. Their clothing may be hiding something, or it may reveal they don't belong in the location they're in.

*One of the best pre-attack indicators is **position**.* For a predator to attack you, he'll need to get close. When there are few people around, it's entirely abnormal for a stranger to get too close to you. So when a stranger attempts to invade your personal space, particularly when there are few people around, it may be a pre-attack indicator. He may also be testing your boundaries or attempting to establish dominance. Other pre-attack indicators are obvious. When a person begins raising his voice, yelling at you, turning red, making big movements, and being otherwise aggressive, he may be gearing up for an attack.

Look, See, and Learn

Warning signs and pre-attack indicators are always there. Once you know what to look for, once you begin paying attention, you'll see them. I'm from New Orleans, a city with lots of tourism. For years I lived in *the* place were all tourists go, the French Quarter. My family lives there today, and I still spend a significant amount of time there. Like many other places with large numbers of tourists, there are predators looking for victims. I've often walked the streets or sat on my balcony, watching them operate.

They stand stationary and watch, where the vast majority of people are walking to and from shops, restaurants, and sights. They position themselves so people will have to walk close to them. Or, they approach strangers immediately putting a hand out for a hand shake, or putting an arm around a stranger's back. Once they get close, they start with a variety of cons, either to get money without physical violence, or to get people to a more isolated location where they can rob them away from witnesses.

Most people are afraid to say "no" when a hustler puts his hand out for a hand shake. It's rude not to reciprocate, and the hustlers rely on that social convention to get close and establish control. For the few people who do refuse, the hustler usually acts offended, accusing the person of racism. And at that point, he gains control again as the victim does everything they can to convince the hustler they're not a racist.

Pay attention to your surroundings, how people behave, what they're looking at, and where they position themselves in relation to others. You may be surprised by how much you're able to see.

3.2.4 How to Prevent the Attack

If you have failed to avoid dangerous places, to increase the risks, and to decrease the rewards enough for a predator to choose another victim, and you see pre-attack indicators, it's still not too late to prevent the attacker from succeeding. What's essential to realize in order to maintain control of the situation, is that *you do have a choice, and you must make that choice*.

In Rob Redenbach's book, *Self Defense In 30 Seconds*, he does an excellent job categorizing the choices along with their pros and cons. I've changed the order of the choices in a way that makes more sense to me:

- **Ignore or Leave**: If possible, you should escape.

- **Dominate**: Verbally and with body language, you dominate the situation, letting the attacker know he has made a mistake, and needs to choose an easier target.

- **Comply**: If your attacker has a weapon, giving him what he wants may be the smartest self defense move there is.

- **Stun and Run**: Nail the attacker, and escape to safety as quickly as possible.

- **Incapacitate**: You attack the attacker until he is completely incapacitated.

- **Restrain**: You control and restrain the attacker.

By making one of the above choices, even if an attacker has already approached you, even if he has threatened to use violence, and even if he has pulled a weapon, you can still maintain or regain control. But you must realize you have that choice, and again, you must purposefully make it. Without making the choice, you *give* your attacker control. There's a great quote from Sun Tzu's *Art of War* that applies here:

> *"To secure ourselves against defeat lies in our own hands, but the opportunity for defeating the enemy is provided by the enemy himself. Hence the saying: One may **know** how to conquer without being able to **do** it."*

Your attacker cannot successfully attack you unless you provide him that opportunity. He cannot control you without you allowing him to do so. The choice is yours, but only if you know that it is. I can't over-emphasize how important it is that you remain in control and make purposeful choices, *even if the choice is to comply*. Stop, and think about this for a while.

Since this chapter focuses on prevention, I'll cover the first three choices (*leaving*, *dominating*, and *complying*) here. The rest of this book will cover the second three, which fall under physical self defense.

3.2.5 Distance Is Prevention

Distance removes *opportunity* from the attacker's equation. It can be used to avoid or escape (*leaving*, in the previous list of choices) from a potential attack. Maintaining a safe distance, such that a potential threat will need to take at least a few steps in order to reach you, is crucial. It isn't realistic to assume you can maintain a safe distance from all people at all times, but it's also unnecessary to do so. In the company of friends, there is no need to maintain a safe distance. In a crowded place, under normal circumstances and where there are no warning signs or pre-attack indicators, it's also unnecessary (and impossible) to maintain distance. But when you're in an isolated area, see warning signs, pre-attack indicators, or don't feel right, you should strive to create as much distance as possible between yourself and any potential threat.

In isolated areas, you should also keep a safe distance from places an attacker may hide in order to surprise you. Keep your distance from recessed doorways and corners, and walk on the side of the street where there are no cars. If someone is approaching and on track to cross your path, cross the street or change direction. Run if you need to.

If you've already been approached by a potential attacker, your first choice is still to escape or leave *as long as you can do so safely*. The key is to do it under the right circumstances, with the right attitude, and at the right time. Many predators will "interview" potential victims, asking questions, violating distance, and watching to see how the target responds. At the interview stage, especially in areas where witnesses are present, where the predator will need to get you to an isolated area first, leaving can be a sign of uncooperativeness, a sign that you will not comply or make a good victim. But in an isolated area where the predator already has the opportunity to attack, leaving may make that opportunity even more attractive. So the key to leaving as a purposeful strategy, is only to use it during the interview stage, as a sign of active noncompliance.

Another very important point to keep in mind when walking away from a threat, no matter where you are or how many people are around, is to maintain your awareness of the threat's position and location. Keep your eye on the threat to make sure he's not coming up behind you. Leaving may seem obvious, but if you don't purposefully make the choice, you may not do it. Social conventions or fear may stop you from leaving when you should. Understand that leaving is your first choice, and make it whenever you can. In the coming section on de-escalation, I'll cover another element of effective leaving, dominating your opponent verbally and with body language.

3.2.6 Evasion

Sometimes, creating enough distance to be completely safe is impossible. It may be that you're far away from safety, and running will put you in a worse position. In these cases, evasion, a close relative of distance, can be a viable option. If you see a potential attacker before he sees you, you may be able to hide. Hiding can be easier than you might imagine. If the potential attacker isn't paying close enough attention, you can make yourself disappear by crouching next to a car or hiding behind a tree, for example.

You might be surprised how easy it is to hide in the open. As long as someone can't see or hear you, you're effectively invisible. As a teenager, I went through a phase where I was pursued on numerous occasions by various people with bad intentions. It wasn't pleasant, but I've been just a couple of feet away from people who were actively looking for me. The key to hiding successfully is to either be safe and secure in your hiding place, or to remain mobile, to circle the object you're hiding behind if the potential attacker is moving such that it becomes necessary. In isolated areas, where you'll most likely need to use evasion, it's even easier, as you don't have to worry about anyone else seeing you and revealing your position.

You can use evasion with cover even if your attacker does see you, as long as he doesn't have a projectile weapon (gun, pepper spray, etc.) that he is willing to use. If you're as fast as your attacker and have good endurance (it is far more tiring than you might imagine), you can play the circle game, circling a parked car for example, while yelling for help. Few attackers who mean you serious harm will chase you around and around a car while you're yelling for help and drawing attention to them.

Unfortunately, evasion may be difficult or impossible if you're with family or friends who aren't on the same page.

3.2.7 De-Escalation

When you can't avoid a potential attacker through avoidance, escape, or evasion, de-escalation is the next best option. In terms of the choices you must make when faced with a threat, *leaving*, *dominating*, and *complying* can all be effective forms of de-escalation.

Every attack requires an escalation of some sort. The escalation may be more or less visible, but it will include a final closing of distance, it may include a verbal escalation, and it may include an "interview", where the perpetrator goes through a process of questioning (verbally and/or non-verbally) the target to confirm his likelihood of success. The perpetrator may also tell the target to do something, and in some cases, *complying* can de-escalate the situation, preventing it from going physical.

Verbal Compliance

Before many attacks, especially when robbery or violence isn't the primary motive, a verbal escalation may occur first, where tension is noticeably built up leading to a physical assault. A typical build up many people will be familiar with is where one male challenges another by saying something like "You got a problem?", or "What are you looking at?". If the answer is "Yeah, you're my problem.", or, "I'm looking at you, asshole!", then the escalation generally progresses until physical violence occurs. But often, simply saying, "I'm sorry man, I didn't mean to stare.", and following such a course, will be enough to stop the escalation and prevent the attack. Sometimes, it will take a couple of *deflective statements*, but by allowing the perpetrator to maintain his dominant role, there will be no need for violence. This is a form of compliance, as you're allowing the perpetrator to maintain or increase his status. Simply leaving can also work in such situations, especially if you do so in a compliant manner.

In the case of violence for conflict resolution, where an argument usually precedes a physical attack, you can also comply by letting your opponent win. Don't participate in escalating the situation further. Saying something like, "Well, you could definitely be right. I need to think about this a little more.", for example, can both end the escalation and the discussion. If you feel a person is beginning to feel provoked by something you're doing or saying, reverse course and/or leave.

Verbal and Physical Dominance

If you feel threatened by someone that you think may want to rob, attack, or abduct you, *dominating* the situation and leaving can work very well during the interview stage, or as the predator is attempting to close the distance. One of the best ways to de-escalate an attack using physical and verbal dominance without physical contact, is to put both hands up as a barrier, create distance, and say in a very loud, commanding voice, "BACK OFF!". *Doing so **absolutely** requires practice.* I'll repeat that. ***Doing so absolutely requires practice.*** We are not socially conditioned to yell at a stranger *before* being physically attacked. Most adults aren't accustomed to yelling at all. It takes practice to say "Back off!" in a loud, commanding voice, to mean it without looking scared or self conscious. If it's not practiced, and if it's not meant and done in a dominating way, such an attempt will come across as weak and fearful. It will have the opposite effect. Practicing establishing distance, putting your hands up as a barrier, ready to attack, and giving the "back off" command is a valuable exercise.

A loud command can be literally stunning. A potential attacker will not expect you to yell at him before he attacks. It will be unexpected, and it will shock him. It will serve to show him you're not a good target, are unwilling to cooperate, draw attention to what he's doing, or give you the time to attack while he is taken off guard.

Exercise: You may need to make sure no one is going to think you're in trouble before you do this, depending on where you live or who you live with. But if you can, scream as loud as you can. Most adults are not used to screaming, and this exercise will help with removing inhibitions.

Physical Compliance

If the threat of violence has already been made, if you were taken unaware and by surprise, especially where deadly weapons are involved, *compliance* is one of the safest choices a person can make. If a predator puts a gun in your face and demands your wallet, your money, your keys, etc., giving him what he's asking for is highly likely to de-escalate the situation. This is difficult for many self defense and martial arts practitioners to accept. They train hard to be able to take out an opponent, and feel that giving a predator what he wants is giving up, or losing. But the goal of self defense is not to beat up, incapacitate, or take out an attacker. The goal of self defense is to survive and prosper, minimizing injury or damage. And the best way to do that when faced with a deadly threat, where giving up a physical object will end that threat, is to comply.

Compliance is an *active* choice. As hard as it might be to accept, it's often the smartest choice you can make, far smarter than resistance. It's very important to realize this. You should practice giving up your money against a deadly threat.

Of course, when a predator wants you or your family, compliance is not a good option, especially when the predator's goal is the act of violence or murder. You can and should try to escape or use verbal and physical dominance at the interview stage if possible, but even with the threat of deadly force, complying is not a de-escalation strategy in such situations. If a predator points a gun at your head and tells you to get in his car, come with him, go inside your house, etc., it's highly unlikely to end well. Your chances are probably much better choosing to sprint away as fast as you can instead of complying. If you can't safely escape, this is where the line between de-escalation and physical self defense is crossed. *If there is one rule in self defense, it is never to comply with a predator who wants **you**.*

3.3 The OODA Loop

The OODA Loop is a concept developed by US Air Force Colonel John Boyd. OODA stands for *Observe, Orient, Decide,* and *Act.* The concept describes the process humans go through when confronted with a stimulus that requires action or decision making. First, we *observe* a stimulus. Second, we *orient* ourselves to the stimulus or new situation. Third, we *decide* what to do based on that observation. And finally, we *act.* The OODA Loop has important implications for self defense strategy.

Normal human interactions can be seen as chains of OODA loops, where one person acts, the other observes, orients, decides, and acts, and the cycle repeats. But in aggressive situations, it's possible for a person to get stuck between the first two phases of the loop. When a predator launches a surprise attack and keeps the pressure on, the victim is bombarded with so much information that they're stuck observing and continuously attempting to orient. They can't even get to the decision phase since the situation is moving and changing at such a quick and overwhelming pace. The predator is in the action phase, and the victim is stuck two steps behind, unable to catch up.

The OODA Loop concept sheds light on why it's so important to be aware of your surroundings, to have a plan, and to proactively make choices. By being aware of your surroundings a potential attacker will be unable to act without you seeing it coming. By making certain choices, *you* are acting, forcing the predator into the first half of the loop, where you are now two steps ahead or at least on the same level as the predator.

This is one reason why using the "Back off!" command is so effective. The predator thinks he has the situation under control. He's decided what he wants to do to you, is in the middle of his plan/action, and all of a sudden you break into his loop. It kicks him back into the observe and orient phases and changes the game. You've taken control, the predator feels it, and is likely to back down, at least momentarily. If you've done so in a place where other people are around, when the predator observes the new situation, he'll quickly realize that all attention is on him, which is a very uncomfortable prospect if he knows he's about to try something illegal. At the least, breaking into the predator's OODA loop will give you the upper hand if you need to resort to physical self defense.

In addition to the "Back off!" command, there are a number of ways to break into a predator's OODA loop, either making him reconsider his attack or making him miss his opportunity. If you're carrying a weapon when you notice a threat, especially in an isolated area, putting your hand on the weapon, drawing the weapon, or disengaging a safety on the weapon, where the potential threat notices your movement, can make him reconsider. Faking a *weapon check* when you don't have one can also work well.

Recently a friend of mine related the following incident to me: He was in a busy tourist area, and needed to make a trip to a hardware store that was about four blocks away. The two blocks closest to the hardware store are relatively deserted, and places where criminals often rob people who park there or transit through them...a perfect "in-between place". My friend noticed three young guys who fit the profile for robbers in the area, walking toward him on the other side of the street, looking around for witnesses, and then looking him over. Although he didn't have a weapon, when they looked at him, he looked right back and pretended to put his hand on a weapon underneath his shirt, as if he was carrying a concealed handgun. He told me they instantly changed their demeanor, quit looking at him, and continued on their way. He told me he's used this tactic on multiple occasions, and it's always worked well. Of course, a fake *weapon check* can backfire, and you should be prepared for that eventuality (to run, to use evasive manoeuvres, to comply, or to fight if necessary). But it's a good example of breaking into a predator's OODA loop and changing his plans without the use of physical violence.

Another strategy that can work to disrupt an opponent's OODA loop, is simply to talk to him, to address him or ask him a question. It's difficult not to at least quickly consider a question when asked, and this can throw an opponent off. Maintaining or creating distance is a safer bet, but if a threat is coming near you, confidently saying "Hey, how are you doing?" can reset his mind and throw off his timing, if not his plan. It's surprising how effective a simple question can be at disrupting a physical plan, if used at the right moment. Next time you're training with a partner, ask him a question right before you attack, and watch what happens. Even after you've done it once or twice, it can still have a surprising effect.

On the other hand, if a predator is "adrenalized", focused, and firmly moving in for the attack, he likely won't even hear whatever question you're asking, making it ineffective.

3.4 Preventing The Freeze

As mentioned in the previous section, a surprise attack can cause a person to freeze, as a fast, overwhelming attack can be too much information for the mind to orient to. Fear can also cause the freeze. And the combination of fear and an overwhelming attack, even worse. In *Facing Violence*, Rory Miller devotes a chapter to different types of freezes and how to break them. I don't have enough experience with freezing or breaking freezes to go into specific examples and details for each type, but two strategies that have worked for me follow the solutions Rory offers.

The nature of a freeze is that you're "frozen", or not doing anything. And it's triggered by someone or something else that is doing something. The key to preventing the freeze (and breaking a freeze) is to *actively* do something. This may seem obvious, but there's more to it, as described below, and it should be a fundamental part of your self defense strategy.

3.4.1 Pre-Positioning

Most predators will attempt to take their victims by surprise. And when you get nailed by an assault you didn't see coming, you will at least momentarily freeze. Everyone will. First, your body and mind will be shocked by the physical nature of the assault. Second, you'll either be completely paralysed on a primal level, stuck trying to figure out what's going on, or you'll pause for a moment while you switch from your everyday mind to a more aggressive state. During this period, you may very well be getting mauled by your attacker. One way to prevent this from happening is to use what I call *pre-positioning*.

Pre-positioning requires you to be aware of the threat before the situation goes physical. Ideally, you'll position yourself far, far away, and there won't be a physical attack at all. But when you can't avoid the threat, (and he's closing in on you) *pre-positioning* involves becoming the predator yourself, mentally and physically. You *pre-position* yourself to attack the threat. Mentally switching from being a victim to being a predator, makes all the difference in the world. *Pre-positioning* is active. It involves doing something. And doing something is the opposite of freezing.

Anyone who has sparred just a bit, standing and with strikes, knows that standing flat footed, chest to chest, with your hands down, and directly in front of your opponent is a very bad idea. But circling to the outside of your opponent, for example, minimizing his options while maximizing your own, works well. *Pre-positioning* involves setting up your position relative to your opponent, and seeing your opponent as your prey rather than as your attacker. If he moves to attack, he's giving you something. He's creating an opening that you will use to your advantage.

You'll need to practice *pre-positioning* in order to understand and use it, but it should be part of your physical martial arts and self defense training. Sparring will help with your ability to *pre-position*, and it will be covered in later chapters on the *Fundamental Five* and *Environmental Applications*.

3.4.2 Conditioned Default Responses

The second strategy, conditioning effective default responses to various types of attacks, is a last ditch option when you are attacked by surprise. If you've conditioned yourself to unconsciously respond to a physical assault, even if you are surprised by the attack, your body will execute the conditioned response. Immediately after the response, you may freeze as you try to figure out what just happened. Hopefully, your training will kick in and you'll continue to act as quickly as possible. I'll cover conditioned responses in detail in the chapters on Functional Training and the Fundamental Five.

3.5 Violence, Danger, And Paranoia

This chapter and the previous one cover serious topics: The nature of violence and its prevention. The material isn't light or nice. It is important however, and it can save your life. With that said, for most people reading this book, the world is a safe and enjoyable place. Physical violence can happen, but for the majority of people in first world countries, it's an exception. The purpose of the material in these two chapters isn't to have you focus on danger or become paranoid. It's to give you the knowledge to avoid or prevent violence without having to use physical self defense.

At first you may need to practice to modify your behavior and become more aware of your environment. But in time, these behaviors will become second nature. You won't need to think about them. Prevention is about minimizing your risks. And when you've done that, when you're well prepared, there will be little to worry about.

As always, there are exceptions. Some places *are* dangerous. And you may live in one of them. I spent seven years of my adult life living in a neighborhood where physical violence was common. There were multiple shootings directly in front of my house, bullet holes in my roof on two occasions, and every two or three nights my wife and I would hear gunshots. There were turf battles with groups of people fighting each other, drug dealers on two corners within two blocks, a brothel with heavily drugged hookers roaming around, and plenty of unsavory characters. Just before we moved into our house, one of our neighbor's sons was murdered. Just before we moved out, another one was murdered, and then set on fire in his car. Another one of our neighbors, who my wife used to make brownies for, was jailed for murdering two people.

One of the best decisions we ever made was to move. The feeling of living in a new place, where we could walk outside at any time, day or night, with no concern for our safety, was indescribable. We immediately felt the difference in our lives, and it was no small thing. If you're living in a dangerous place or with a dangerous person, it doesn't have to be that way. *Leave*. It might not be easy, but you can make it work, and you'll be glad you did.

Life is too short to be obsessed with violence. Minimize your risks, learn what to watch out for and how to respond if you do get into trouble, and then forget about it.

The best thing about functional self defense and martial arts practice has nothing to do with violence. The best thing is that it's healthy and a great deal of fun. It's fantastic for exercise, incredible for balance, and a physical and mental challenge. The variety and range of movement and force is liberating for your body. You can do it for the rest of your life, and you'll always have room to improve. Stand up, clinch, ground, striking, grappling, blunt objects, sharp objects, and projectiles, with a partner, in a group, or alone, indoors and outdoors, there's a near infinite amount to practice and enjoy.

Take-Aways

- Avoid dangerous places.
- Be a bad target.
- Be aware of your surroundings.
- Watch out for warning signs and pre-attack indicators.
- Maintain a safe distance from potential threats and places they may wait.
- Create layers of security for your home.
- Escape to safety when you feel threatened.
- Evade a threat when you can't completely escape.
- Use the "Back off!" command to dominate the situation if a threat gets close.
- Comply: Give in to an argument or give up your money if it will prevent physical violence.
- Never go anywhere with a predator. Never give him privacy and time with you or your family.
- If a threat is closing in, *pre-position* for your attack. Become the predator, and the predator becomes the victim.

Chapter 4
The Covered Blast

The Covered Blast

The *Covered Blast* is an FSD concept that can dramatically increase your abilities, by maximizing your options while minimizing your opponent's. It can and should be applied to the use of all self defense and martial arts.

Every physical attack includes an *entry*, potential *follow-ups*, and an *exit*. The *entry* consists of the motion of convergence toward an opponent, when the distance is such that it's required, and the first offensive technique used. *Follow-ups* are any techniques that occur after the *entry* and before the *exit*. And the *exit* consists of the motion of divergence, or the motion required to get out of the opponent's fighting range.

The *Covered Blast* is a single concept or strategy that combines a *covered entry*, *covered follow-ups*, and a *covered exit*. Cover equals protection. The purpose of the *covered blast* is to ensure you're protected during the entire duration of an encounter, and are able to attack your opponent while he is unable to attack you.

4.1 Why Cover Is Crucial

In self defense, your primary goal is to avoid getting injured. Taking out your opponent is a secondary goal, which may even be unnecessary in some situations. Consider that it would be better to escape and avoid injury without taking your opponent out, than to take your opponent out but also get injured in the process.

A gun fighting example will illustrate this point very well. Imagine that a person with a gun in concealment is taken by surprise, threatened by an attacker with a gun that is already drawn, and asked to give up his money. If the defender's primary goal is to shoot the attacker, and he reaches for his gun, pulls it out, and fires, he may very well achieve his goal. But he'll probably also get shot in the process. In fact, by focusing so much on offense with no regard for defense, he may end up shot without even having the opportunity to shoot his attacker. From a self defense perspective, from a survival perspective, he would be better off giving the attacker his money. *If* he absolutely needed to shoot the attacker, his first move should include a defensive component, to get control of the weapon and then shoot, to sprint to cover and then shoot, or to give the attacker his money, and shoot him in the back as he leaves (ethics and legality aside).

The concept of the *Covered Blast* is more important than it may seem. Strategy and goals should determine tactics and techniques, not the other way around. If your techniques dictate your strategy, you may get nailed before, during, or after you attempt to apply them.

4.2 What Exactly Is Cover?

Cover is protection. And there are a variety of methods you can use to achieve it. Ideally, you'll use a combination of methods to give you multiple layers of security, making it that much harder for your opponent to break through. But keep in mind that all cover is temporary. Your opponent can and will act to remove your cover, so maintaining it is a continuous effort.

Distance is cover. If you're too far away from your opponent for him to hit you without stepping forward, you're temporarily covered. Like all forms of cover, distance requires the opponent to make an extra movement before attacking. In the case of distance, he must step toward you first.

In the left example you see poor positioning in combination with a finger jab to the eye, allowing gray shirt to strike blue shirt. In the right example, you see good positioning, where blue shirt is largely covered against gray shirt's potential attack.

Position is cover. If you're positioned behind your opponent, to the outside of his reach, on top of him, or in any otherwise superior position, you're temporarily covered. In order for your opponent to attack you from an inferior position, he'll have to change his position first. When you can attack with one movement but your opponent must make at least two, as long as you maintain your position and/or continuously attack, your opponent will always be a step behind. This is especially true in grappling, where inferior positions are slower and more difficult to reverse.

Physical cover is cover. There's a difference between a physical cover and a block. A physical cover works by using part of your body (typically the forearm or lower leg) to guard or protect a vulnerable area from attack, whereas a block diverts an attack. While physical cover alone isn't ideal, combining it with footwork can be an extremely effective way to better your position.

Physical control is cover. If you're holding your opponent in such a way that he cannot attack you without first escaping from the hold, you're temporarily covered. Physical control is especially effective when it allows you to strike, throw, lock, or choke your opponent from a position in which he cannot easily attack you.

Trapping, as it's commonly defined, is a form of physical control with a shorter duration than most grabs and holds. Trapping involves smacking or jerking an opponent's limbs to prevent them from being used for both offense and defense.

Attacking is cover. Launching a hard, continuous, forward pressure attack is one of the best ways to stop your opponent from attacking you. Of course, your opponent can move and counter, so the attack needs to be launched at the right time, and it needs to be overwhelming.

Blocks and deflections are cover. Blocks and deflections are similar to trapping, in the sense that they're techniques of short duration.

The *Covered Blast* utilizes a continuous ***combination*** of distance, position, attacks, physical cover, grabbing, trapping, blocking, and deflecting, to minimize your opponent's ability to attack you, while maximizing your ability to attack him. While all martial arts, combat sports, and self defense systems use some of the techniques above, many do so without an emphasis on staying protected through continuous cover.

4.3 Examples

Here are a few examples that illustrate the use of the *Covered Blast*:

In the images above, blue shirt uses a block typically trained in many traditional martial arts. While the block covers blue shirt against a single technique, the way it is performed (distance and position) in this example leaves blue shirt open to an obvious and likely follow up. It does not follow the principle of the covered blast. Notice however that the FSD crash, below, utilizes a nearly identical block, but with both arms and a lowered head.

In this example, gray shirt uses the same type of block, but with both arms, a lowered head, and with strong forward pressure. This technique combines blocking, covering, and attacking, stopping blue shirt from continuing his attack, and allowing gray shirt to transition to an even better control. This example follows the principle of the covered blast.

In the images above blue shirt uses the FSD Smack and Hack to attack gray shirt, another excellent example of a covered entry. Blue shirt smacks gray shirt's lead/left arm down with a physical control or trap, to prevent gray shirt from using the arm to block or strike. He attacks with a hack to the side of gray shirt's neck, and also drops his head so the attack forms a physical cover that would block or deflect an attack from gray shirt's right hand. Blue shirt is combining a physical control, an attack, and a cover in this entry.

For the covered follow up blue shirt drives gray shirt back and knees him in the groin or solar plexus, all the while maintaining his cover and physical control. He then exits with an elbow strike, from a covered position, below.

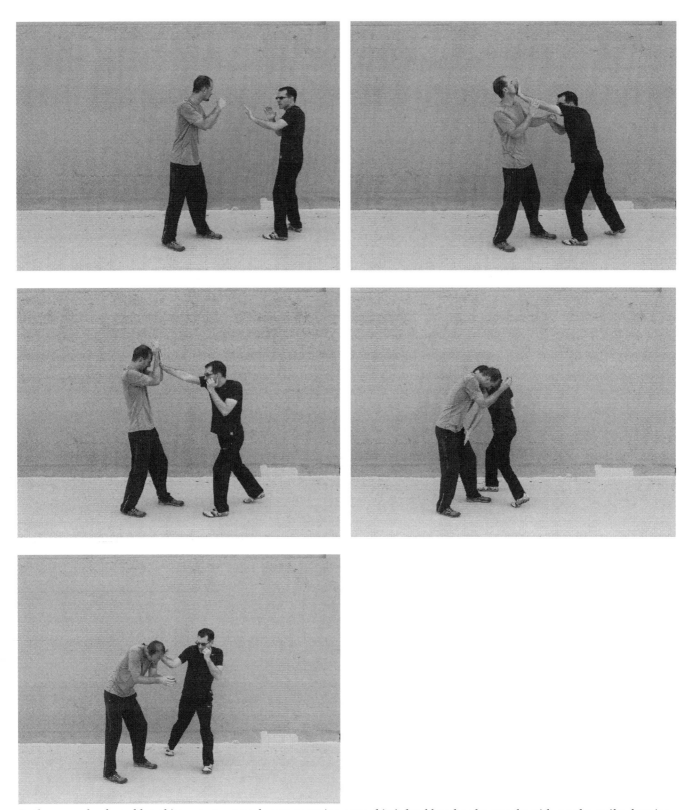

In the example above blue shirt uses a covered entry, trapping gray shirt's lead hand as he attacks with a palm strike, keeping his head low and using the palm strike for cover against gray shirt's rear hand. He continues the attack with a covered follow up, maintaining good cover on the second palm strike, and moving to a superior position on the groin slap. He uses an open hand strike to gray shirt's ear and head to assist in his covered exit from a superior position.

The examples above are staged. Such attacks *may* work exactly as illustrated. But they may not. The use of continuous pressure and cover makes it very difficult for the receiver to mount an effective offense in the face of the *Covered Blast*. But the key to making the *Covered Blast* work is to maintain it in the chaos of a "fight".

Blue shirt zones to the outside and counter punches against gray shirt's attack, but gray shirt shifts toward blue shirt and attacks again. Blue shirt ducks under the second punch with another counter punch from a covered position.

Blue shirt attacks gray shirt trying to keep him on defense, but gray shirt strikes back before blue shirt can continue. Blue shirt steps offline with a cover.

The two examples above demonstrate maintaining a covered position using boxing techniques, even when the encounter doesn't go as desired. Ideally, the aim is to get better control of your opponent as quickly as possible, to decrease his ability to easily counter attack. This is significantly more difficult to do purely with striking, as your opponent can nearly always strike back. A combination of physical control, cover, and striking is ideal, and will be demonstrated in great detail in the coming chapters.

Although weapon use and defense is beyond the scope of this book, in the examples on the next page you can see that the *Covered Blast* can be universally applied, with or without weapons.

Blue shirt uses a covered entry to protect against gray shirt's stick, and also traps his arm. He then strikes gray shirt from a safe position.

Blue shirt evades gray shirts attack with a heavier weapon, using distance as cover. Blue shirt then enters with an attack to gray shirt's arm that takes out his arm and covers his follow up striking angle.

In the rest of this book, notice how the principles of the *Covered Blast* are utilized in all styles and situations. No matter what style you practice, you should be able to use the *Covered Blast*. It may require a modification of techniques, distance, or position, but whatever modifications are necessary to make will make your techniques that much more effective.

Take-Aways

- Avoiding damage is more important than taking out an opponent.
- Use a combination of distance, position, cover, blocking, striking, trapping, and controlling to minimize your risk of damage at *all times*.

Chapter 5
Functional Self Defense Training

Functional Self Defense Training

No matter how effective your techniques are, they are useless without functional training. Functional training gives you the skills necessary to *apply* your techniques, the speed, power, reactions, ability to control distance, timing, and much more, in natural environments and against opponents who are 100% uncooperative.

Most people who practice self defense or martial arts *think* their training is functional, but unfortunately, it's easy for instructors to teach non-functional training methods without even knowing it, particularly when students are not competing in no-rules (or few rules) environments against competitors of different systems. If practitioners only train in a cooperative setting, even if there is resistance, if they aren't having to use their techniques against completely uncooperative opponents of different styles, they may see that their techniques are working in the training room, and not realize that they would not work in the face of a real attack. For this reason, it is important to briefly describe the problems with many common training methods.

5.1 Training Methods And Issues

*First, keep in mind that **no training method is perfect***. Fighting is dangerous, and in a real fight, at least one person is going to get hurt. In order to train safely, we necessarily remove elements from training that are present in a real fight or self defense situation. We remove or limit techniques, slow down, don't go full power, "pull punches", remove the element of surprise, cooperate to an unrealistic degree, use padded training gear and padded or soft weapons. When real elements are removed from training methods, they loses some effectiveness. Unfortunately, we do need all of the elements. Just like a chain, where one weak link will weaken the entire chain, one missing element can negate all of your skills when it comes time to apply them. *The only way to compensate is to have a variety of training methods such that the deficiencies are balanced out*.

It's important to understand the problems with various training methods in order to understand how to balance their weaknesses.

5.1.1 Solo Training

Many martial arts use solo forms (prearranged patterns of techniques, done alone in the air) as a primary training method. Any training method that has a practitioner train alone *cannot* provide comprehensive, functional skills, due to the missing opponent. Solo training can help a practitioner to increase speed, ingrain movements and form, to sharpen focus and concentration, and it can also be great exercise. However, the issue of the missing opponent is ***huge***. Speed is nothing when not in relation to an actual attack. Movements and form are useless when not subject to the pressure of an attack or related to an actual opponent. Focus and concentration are much more challenging in the face of an opponent attempting to hurt you. It doesn't matter how great your solo training exercises are if they're all you're doing. Solo training absolutely cannot prepare you for a real attack against a real opponent.

Any time you have a partner available you should be training with that partner, instead of training solo. Every quality or skill that can be increased in solo training can be increased more effectively through partner training. The only place for solo training is when you feel like training but do not have a partner. Of course, this only pertains to self defense or combat athletics training, as martial arts practiced for fun or health don't need to be functional for self defense.

5.1.2 Cooperative Partner Training

Cooperative drilling with a partner, prearranged or not, is a big step forward along the path toward realistic skills. Again, drilling techniques with a partner can provide you with everything you can get from solo training, plus a whole lot more.

The key to effectiveness for all cooperative partner training is *progressive resistance*. As a beginner, learning a new technique, or just warming up, there is nothing wrong with starting at a slow and relaxed pace. However, a real attack will not be slow and relaxed. It will be fast, hard, and powerful. *Progressive resistance* should be used in all training. As a practitioner becomes comfortable performing a technique at a certain level of speed and power, that level should be increased progressively. Smooth progression is important. Going from slow and relaxed to hard and fast is hardly ever productive, aside from possibly demonstrating the extreme difference between the two modes. The gradual progression however will safely and effectively bring a practitioner to the point where he or she can handle a full power attack with skill and confidence. Cooperative drilling can be prearranged, so you can work on particular techniques or to develop particular skills. On the boxing page of my website, *www.functionalselfdefense.org*, I provide a video of a basic boxing progression with prearranged drills, and later in this book you will find many additional training drills. For example, practitioners can agree to work on a single attack and a single defense, multiple attacks and defenses, or to flow in a non-prearranged way but with limitations.

But cooperative training is not enough. A real opponent or attacker will not be cooperative. A real attacker will try as hard as possible to prevent you from doing what you want. And that doesn't mean the attacker will only resist. There is a significant difference between resistance and being noncooperative. Let's look at an example:

In the pictures above you see blue shirt applying a common "elbow lock" on gray shirt. Gray shirt is entirely cooperative, allowing blue shirt to perform the lock. In many martial art schools, training ends here and the lock is assumed to work.

*In the first image above you see gray shirt resisting the elbow lock. However, he is not entirely uncooperative. He resists, but **he stands still** and allows blue shirt try to apply the lock. In the second image you see an example of uncooperativeness. When blue shirt attempts to apply the lock, gray shirt not only resists, but also punches blue shirt in the face.*

It's very easy to be misled by your own practice, to think your partner is being uncooperative and acting as a real attacker would, even when he is not. In a stylized martial art or self defense class, we quickly become conditioned only to attack in certain ways, only to resist in certain ways, and even to react to our partner's counters in certain ways. It's far more common than most people think, and *nearly everyone, even in competitive combat sports, does this to some degree*. I'll relate an example of this happening to me.

When I was in college, I took an aikido class offered by the university. The classes were three hours long, three times a week. For the first hour we primarily did stretching and warm up exercises, and then break-falls (practice where we learned how to fall without being injured). Every class began with a *lot* of rolling and falling. When we'd move into the second and third hours, when our partners would use an aikido lock or throw, we'd roll or fall out of the technique to avoid being injured or having a joint broken. Or at least, that is what we were told we were doing.

At the time, I was teaching a self defense style that was karate-based. The training was hard core, and included lots of weapon defense practice. Despite it being less than the most efficient and effective system, it had been used successfully in self defense, numerous times, by a significant number of practitioners. I didn't have the knowledge then that I would have later, but I was focused entirely on effective self defense.

I kept my aikido training separate from what I was teaching and training at the self defense school. But 6 months into my aikido practice, I attempted to show an aikido lock to a long time student at the school. It was a wrist lock called *kotegaishi*. The student let me catch his punch, but as soon as I began to apply the lock, he punched me in the face with his other hand. He then told me that there was no way I could ever catch his punch, and even if I could he'd just hit me with the other hand. I figured I just hadn't practiced aikido enough, and that there must be some way the technique would work. Otherwise, why would my aikido instructor be teaching it?

I liked aikido, and I continued going to the classes for a year or so, until another event opened my eyes to how badly I had been conditioned by the practice. About halfway into a class, we were practicing a defensive technique against a two-handed pushing attack. The technique involved redirecting the attacker's arms in such a way that they were twisted, and he was thrown to the floor. Each student would have a turn standing in front of the class, and the rest of the students would line up, attempt to push him, and get thrown to the floor. In the middle of training this technique, a first time student arrived late to the class (the class was mixed with people at a variety of skill levels). As the new student came onto the mat, the teacher was taking a turn demonstrating the technique against all of the students. Each one of us approached the teacher, attempted to push him, and we were promptly and vigorously thrown to the floor. Then, the new student approached the teacher and attempted to push him. The teacher did the technique on the new student, and the only thing that happened was the new guy's arms became a bit crossed. The teacher told him that he needed to fall and roll on the floor to avoid being injured, and the new guy said, "But this won't injure me. You're not doing anything to me." The teacher again told the guy to push him, tried to do the technique harder, and the same thing happened again. Nothing. The teacher told him he wasn't pushing with enough energy. Regardless of how the situation was rearranged, the same thing happened to the new guy. Nothing.

The new guy left and never came back. And after talking to the teacher, so did I. I realized that the aikido training itself had conditioned me to fall and roll, to move away from the pain of a lock in such a way that was not only unnecessary and unrealistic, but that also stopped me from seeing that either the techniques wouldn't work at all, or that there were easy and even natural ways for me to counter them. And I didn't come to this situation as a beginner with no knowledge of martial arts, but as a black belt in a pretty practical style. It's easier to become conditioned than most people think.

The *best* thing about cooperative training is that it's cooperative. It allows you to work on perfecting techniques against a real person. But the *worst* thing about cooperative training is also that it's cooperative. Not only will a real attacker be completely uncooperative, but cooperative training can lead to the use of "fantasy techniques". These techniques work in training, so it seems they will work in self defense or against a real attacker. But they won't.

5.1.3 Sparring
Sparring involves a partner who is both resisting and uncooperative. It's another big step further on the path to functional self defense skills. Moving from cooperative partner training to sparring is like moving from one world to another. At first, if a practitioner has never sparred, he will likely feel like a total beginner.

Sparring can and should be practiced safely. Practitioners should begin at a slow and relaxed pace, and limit techniques and/or ranges. For example, in boxing style sparring practitioners can begin by only sparring with a single punch to a single target, along with a single defense. As they become comfortable with the techniques, they can increase the speed and power, and/or the techniques and ranges allowed.

Sparring is as close as you can get to the randomness and chaos of a real fight or physical self defense situation. However, *safe sparring practice also necessarily lacks other crucial elements of a real fight*. In order to spar without getting injured, practitioners must spar at a lowered intensity, with protective gear, and/or limit damaging techniques in some way. And this can have a more significant impact than it may seem. Many techniques and counters that work well at mid-level intensity will utterly fail in the face of a full intensity attack. Protective gear can make techniques work that wouldn't work otherwise, and prohibit the use of more effective techniques. And limiting techniques prevents both the practitioner and his partner from learning to defend against them.

Some martial arts instructors argue that if you can defend against a boxer's jab, you can defend against an eye strike. If you can defend against a Thai kick to the inner thigh, you can defend against a groin kick. But an eye jab and a groin kick require far less force to do damage, can be thrown quicker, and from additional angles. Failing to train against these techniques may mean you're unable to defend against them in reality.

5.1.4 Random Flowing

Random flowing, is a bridge between cooperative drilling and sparring. (See Maija Soderholm's work for much more on random flowing.) It includes elements of randomness *and* cooperation. In sparring the goal is to beat your opponent. In random flowing the goal is for both you and your partner to help each other learn. Random flowing can have many forms and variations. A simple example might be one-for-one attack and counter attack flowing, where person X launches a single attack, person Y counters that attack with a single counter, person X then counters the counter, person Y then counters that counter, and so on. Alternatively, person X could launch a single attack and allow Y to counter with a combination attack (where person X blocks or avoids the combination but does not counter), and then switch roles over and over again.

The design of a random flow exercise is entirely based on the training goal. However, there must be some random element to it. Otherwise, it is simply a prearranged, cooperative partner drill. If two practitioners wanted to work on defending against a jab, they could begin with a prearranged exercise where person X only throws jabs and person Y trains single or multiple defenses. This would not fall under random flowing, as there is no real random element to the exercise. To make the exercise random, person X must be allowed to use at least two different attacks, where person Y does not know which attack will be coming.

5.1.5 The Greater Whole

In the case of mixing training methods, the whole is greater than the sum of its parts. By mixing prearranged cooperative drilling, random flowing, and sparring, a practitioner is able to cover the deficiencies of each training method with the advantages of another.

There is nothing like training at 100% intensity. It is necessary to experience the speed and power of a real attack, to be accustomed to pushing at 100%, and defending against attacks that come in at 100%. It also allows you to push to and extend your limits. But it can't be done safely and in an unlimited manner in sparring. So we use prearranged cooperative training to train at full intensity. But cooperative training is lacking the random element of a real fight. So we use sparring to cover the random element. And, random flowing acts as a bridge to better learn to apply techniques in sparring or fighting. The combination is the key.

Unfortunately, there are still many martial arts and self defense schools that leave out one or more of the above training methods, and/or under utilize what they do train. Some styles only use a combination of solo forms and prearranged drilling. Their practitioners will likely be unprepared for the random nature of a real fight. Some systems train primarily in a random fashion, using low intensity sparring, and leave out full speed and power training. Their practitioners will likely be overwhelmed by the power of a real attack. Other systems train both random and hard, but leave out techniques or rely on training gear for safety. Their practitioners may get nailed by techniques they've never trained defending against. Using the right combination of training methods avoids these shortfalls.

5.2 The "I Method"

The *I Method* is a great model developed by Matt Thornton, that makes it easy to incorporate all of the previous training methods. There are three phases: *Introduction*, *Isolation*, and *Integration*.

Introduction: When a practitioner first learns a technique, he or she is at the *introduction* phase. This phase typically only lasts a few minutes. It's just long enough for the practitioner to learn the basic physical mechanics of a movement or technique. It is *not* the phase where the practitioner becomes skilled at a technique or "perfects" it. It is simply as it implies, an introduction.

Isolation: The second phase is *isolation*, where a technique is practiced in an isolated or limited environment to achieve a higher level of skill with it. This is the phase at which cooperative partner training is useful. A practitioner takes a technique and trains it within the context it is meant for, with a partner who is applying progressive resistance. The *isolation* phase is where practitioners can train to develop qualities at full speed and power, since there is still a level of cooperation to keep training safe. Solo training can also be useful here (when a partner is not available), as can applying techniques against focus mitts, padded shields, or hanging bags (where it applies). Since random flowing is a bridge between cooperative training and sparring, it can also be used in the *isolation* phase, to bridge to the third phase.

Integration: The third phase is *integration*. In this phase the practitioner integrates the technique into live use or sparring, eventually in a technically unlimited environment. It's one thing to be able to use a counter, for example, when you know your partner is going to throw a straight punch with his left hand. It's another thing when you have no idea if he's even going to throw a punch at all. This is what the *integration* phase is for. It can and should be entered into progressively, and random flowing is a good way to do that.

Boxing is a system with relatively few techniques, and can provide a simple example of the use of the *I Method*. A practitioner may learn a jab (lead hand punch) and a catch (simple defense), and train only those techniques with a partner (isolated). Then the practitioner learns a cross (rear hand punch) and a cover (another simple defense), and trains them in isolation. For the *integration* phase, the practitioners can use the jab or the cross, the catch or the cover. They may begin with random flowing, where one of them attacks and the other defends, and then they switch roles. And finally, they progress to sparring, where either of them can attack at any time.

The same basic progression can be used with the hook, uppercut, parries, ducks, etc. Kicking and kicking defenses can be added. Stand up grappling can be added. Ground grappling can be added. Strikes can be added to ground fighting. Weapons can be added, and so on. Each technique is introduced, trained in isolation, and then integrated into the mix. It must be that way. Otherwise, if a technique is not integrated into random, live training, it will be exceedingly difficult to apply it in reality.

5.2.1 Random Flow, Sparring, And Integration Progressions

In my experience both teaching and training, I've noticed that practitioners have a hard time if they take a number of techniques from the isolation phase and are then thrown into sparring with all of the techniques as options. *It's easier to learn to use a technique, or to learn to apply it more efficiently and effectively, when there are fewer variables in the mix.*

Many traditional martial arts schools make this mistake. Practitioners learn numerous techniques that they train in solo forms. Then they practice them in very limited, isolated drills. And then they are told to "go spar". What ends up happening is just a sloppy mess. They haven't yet learned to apply their techniques with confidence and skill, and they're never going to with such a "method". Their solo and prearranged training ends up looking completely different from their sparring. The solo and prearranged training looks like "martial arts", and the sparring looks like two people playing tag with messy punches, kicks, and blocks.

The way to avoid this from happening is to slowly integrate techniques, one by one, into the mix. At first, the mix is very small, only including a couple of techniques. In time, it expands to include all techniques in the practitioners repertoire. Tactics and strategies can also be progressively added to the mix. For example, one practitioner can work on attacking, and another can work on counter attacking. One practitioner can work on striking, and another can work on entering to the clinch without getting hit.

When everything is on the table too soon, it becomes more difficult to improve on specific techniques and skills, to consistently apply a particular tactic or strategy. But by progressively integrating techniques, tactics, and strategies, it becomes much easier. The design of a training session should be based on the goals of the practitioners. If the goal is to learn to stop a grappler with striking, then you may start with only one take down or clinch entry, and progressively add more. If the goal is to better your defense against striking, then start with only one punch and progressively add more.

51

5.3 The Mixed Martial Arts (MMA) Base

The *MMA Base* is the foundation of comprehensive, functional self defense, and is the ideal mix to begin training with. It includes the most common striking and wrestling techniques in all ranges (stand up, clinch, and ground), but even more importantly, it utilizes the most efficient and effective base from which to execute these techniques. The *MMA Base* teaches fundamental skills in attack and defense, including not only particular techniques, but the ability to move and to manipulate distance, position, and timing to your advantage.

The *MMA Base* is primarily made up of boxing, Thai boxing, stand-up wrestling, and Brazilian jiu jitsu. It is not necessary for a self defense practitioner to become an "expert" in any of these systems (although that certainly wouldn't be a bad thing!). What is important is for a practitioner to have the fundamentals of each system solidly down. Every practitioner interested in comprehensive physical self defense ability must know how to punch and defend against punches, to kick and defend against kicks, and to wrestle standing and on the ground. These techniques are what humans naturally use to attack, and the "delivery systems" or base used in the *MMA Base* is the most natural and intuitive base from which to attack.

Are the techniques in the various *MMA Base* systems the most efficient and effective for self defense? Very often, the answer is no. Boxing and Thai boxing use close fisted punches to the head for example, and punching the head is not ideal in self defense. It's more likely that such a technique will result in a broken hand than an unconscious attacker. High kicks are also a very bad idea in self defense, yet they are used in Thai boxing. There are many more examples. But the point of *MMA Base* training is not necessarily to use the techniques exactly as they're used in the *MMA Base* systems, but to learn how to use and defend against them (if you can't use them, your partner can't practice defending against them), and to have a safe base from which to practice "fighting".

Burton Richardson has a great saying, "If you want to learn how to fight, you must practice against someone who is fighting back." *That*, primarily, is what the *MMA Base* is for.

The MMA Base Progression

The next chapter will be the start of the technical part of this book, and in it I will lay out the systems of the *MMA Base*, alone with the necessary techniques and training methods for each. My preference is to begin with boxing, add kicks, knees, and elbows, then add stand up wrestling (first without strikes and then adding strikes), and then add wrestling on the ground (again, first without strikes and then adding them). This progression brings a practitioner from stand-up "unattached" fighting to ground fighting in a logical way. However, there is no reason I'm aware of as to why a practitioner couldn't start with ground fighting and work their way up, or stand up wrestling and work out to striking and then down to the ground. Any approach can work, as long as all the "ranges" are trained.

5.4 Self Defense: Beyond The MMA Base

The techniques and systems of the *MMA Base* are designed primarily for one-on-one sport based fights between people in similar weight classes, in an area designed for safe fighting, where both participants know what is about to happen. There are rules that prohibit some of the most effective and damaging techniques from being used, and by removing those techniques from the equation, unique and effective footwork, perfect for self defense, is also neglected. For the most efficient and effective physical self defense, we must go beyond the *MMA Base*.

5.4.1 Self Defense Techniques

Many techniques from the *MMA Base* are excellent for self defense. Some need to be modified slightly, and others need to be scrapped all together. In addition, techniques that are not a part of the *MMA Base* should be added to a practitioner's repertoire. Chapter 7 will cover this in detail.

5.4.2 Natural Environments

One of the most overlooked problems with martial arts and self defense training is the fact that training is done in clean, empty, temperature regulated, often padded, and well lit rooms. The majority of natural environments are *very* different, and this has a significant impact on fighting in them.

Outdoors, in cities, there are buildings, parked cars, and curbs nearly everywhere. There are moving cars coming down streets, garbage cans, street signs, light posts, parking meters, cracked sidewalks, plants, trees, etc.. What distinguishes the average public area from an open field are all the "things", which are all over the place! Weather can have a significant impact on the ground. Depending on the weather there may be snow, or the ground may be wet and slippery due to rain. When it's hot, people may be sweaty. When it's cold, they may have thick jackets on. The ground may be rocky, very hard, and rough. Outside of cities, the ground will be uneven, often with holes and rocks, and full of plants and trees.

Indoors, there are similar issues. There are desks, tables, chairs, sofas, benches, and walls everywhere. There are numerous objects to trip over or get shoved into. There is very often limited space. Indoors and outdoors, there may be people in your way. It may be dark. There are plenty of objects that can be used against you, or that you can use against your opponent.

If you've only trained in a gym or dojo specifically set up for safe training, attempting to fight in a natural environment will be eye opening. In cooperative training where you don't use your environment, you'll have to be careful not to run into certain things, or to run your partner into them. When you're making use of your environment, you'll quickly realize how easy it is to back your partner over an object so he trips and falls, or to slam him into a pointy corner, desk, tree, or car. In wrestling, there are surfaces you just won't want to wrestle on, because they'll be too painful. In a hallway, you won't have room to turn around on the ground. In a public bathroom stall, you won't be able to do anything on the ground at all. Just going there will likely mean someone breaks something as they get slammed onto the solid toilet.

My preference is to train outdoors, regardless of the weather. For functional self defense, you need to be able to fight in the cold, heat, rain, and snow (depending on the environments you live and travel in). Each poses different problems, and has different advantages and disadvantages. Snow is easier to slip and fall on, but it also makes landings soft. Ice is easy to slip on, and it hurts when you fall on it. Training in thick coats is different from training in t-shirts.

In addition to outdoor training, you should also spend some time training indoors, in natural environments. It's difficult to do this hard, as you won't want to break things. And if you're fighting at a high level of intensity, things *will* get broken. But you can do slower indoor training in a variety of different natural environments, and take note of all the things you'll need to watch out for, what you can use, and what you have to avoid being used against you. Keep in mind that nearly anything can be thrown at an opponent to provide a great distraction before either nailing him with something else, or escaping.

I find training in the woods to be close to indoor training in terms of the amount of "stuff" you have to watch out for. And the nice thing about training in woods, aside from nature, is that you don't have to worry about breaking anything other than yourself or your partner. If you train martial arts or self defense regularly, but haven't tried training in natural environments, do it! You'll be glad you did.

5.4.3 Adrenal Issues

In a real self defense situation, your body will release epinephrine and adrenaline into your blood stream, a natural biological response to danger or fear. At lower release levels, adrenaline can increase your ability to perform, but at higher release levels, although you may be able to perform with increased speed and strength, your fine motor skills will be vastly degraded. At higher release levels, you won't be able to perform many common martial arts or self defense moves.

In my opinion, it's unlikely that a practitioner can learn to use fine motor skills under a high level adrenaline dump. Once a significant amount of adrenaline has been released into your system, it will degrade your skills. Therefore, the primary goal is to avoid a full adrenaline dump by avoiding surprise and staying as calm as possible. The more you engage in a particular activity, the more accustomed you become to it. If you've never experienced sparring and getting punched in the face, it *will* surprise you when it happens for the first time. It will shock you, and it will degrade your ability to function. As the saying goes, you'll forget everything you know. If you have experienced sparring however, and you have experienced getting punched, kicked, and wrestled, you'll be less likely to be shocked or surprised if it happens outside of training. You'll be accustomed to the feeling, and you'll be accustomed to performing immediately after.

A real self defense situation is different from training, however. There will be an increased level of fear, and especially if surprise is involved, there will be an increased adrenaline dump. Minimizing surprise is crucial, and that can be achieved through awareness and pre-positioning (covered in Chapters 3 and 8).

An adrenaline dump can make you feel trapped. It will increase your heart rate and breathing, and can lead to a panicked feeling that can feed on itself. Fear can increase fear. Training that either causes an adrenaline dump or simulates the effects is extremely useful in getting as accustomed as possible to it, helping to stay calm and minimize the add-on effect. There are a few drills that work well to simulate the effects of an adrenaline dump, but they must be approached carefully and should be overseen by a qualified instructor.

Exhaustion Training: In this drill a practitioner does a very taxing exercise over and over again until he is unable to continue. Performing burpees, sprints, or hitting targets until exhaustion are good examples. When the practitioner reaches the point at which they can no longer continue, they're attacked by their training partner and must fight back. A training partner or instructor who yells and screams at the practitioner can increase the impact of the drill.

Multiple Opponent Training: A variety of multiple opponent training exercises can provoke an even stronger response than one-on-one exhaustion training. One common version involves a practitioner standing in the middle of a circle of other practitioners, who all attack at the same time, where the practitioner must fight back until they can no longer do so. In another common version, the setup is the same, but the circle of attackers slam the practitioner with padded kicking shields, and the practitioner must repeatedly punch the shields. Both drills sound easier than they are and should be approached carefully. When pushed hard, both drills will trigger a full adrenaline dump. When pushed too hard, the "man in the middle" can end up urinating on himself and/or having a temporary break down. It's important for an experienced instructor to oversee this kind of training and stop the exercise before it goes too far. In both drills all participants should wear padded head gear and gloves.

Head gear helps to simulate an adrenaline dump by minimizing peripheral vision. It also helps to make the practitioner feel trapped. At the end of any of the above drills, if the practitioner is wearing head gear, he or she will have an intense desire to rip it off. The head gear should be left on however, until the practitioner can become calm and relaxed.

5.4.4 Meditation

Meditation will be covered at the end of this book, but should be briefly mentioned here. Many forms of meditation involve a focus on breathing that leads to a calm and relaxed awareness. When a practitioner first begins to meditate, it will take many practice sessions to attain a deep calm and relaxed awareness. The more a practitioner meditates, the quicker he or she will be able to get into this state, and the longer it will last after the specific practice has ended. Over time, the practitioner will develop a relaxation response, where controlled breathing will instantly trigger the optimal state of calm and relaxed awareness.

This relaxation response can be purposefully used in times of fear, to minimize the adrenaline dump and maximize performance. It applies equally well in the above mentioned adrenal training exercises. In my view, it is more beneficial for a practitioner to attain some level of skill in meditation before engaging in adrenal training, in order to give them the skills to effectively manage it. Again, meditation will be covered in the last chapter of this book.

5.4.5 Multiple Opponents

Fighting one attacker is hard enough. Fighting more than one is nearly impossible without better strategy, better weapons, and/or a serious dose of luck. You cannot effectively fight more than one opponent if they are simultaneously fighting back, unless they are ridiculously week, slow, and unskilled. You will be taking damage. So the key to dealing with multiple opponents is to fight them one at a time, to situate yourself such that only one can attack you at any one time. It is possible to do this, if you're facing two opponents for example, by quickly taking one of them out, so there is only one remaining. However, if this is your *only* strategy, it makes the dangerous assumption that your initial attack will be successful. What happens if your attack doesn't take the first opponent out? What if he blocks or grabs you? If your initial attack fails and you're in the middle of two opponents, you're going to be in a world of trouble.

In multiple opponent training and scenarios, footwork is your friend. Your goal should be to use footwork to get to the outside of the group, to line up the opponents so that the one you're dealing with is blocking the others from attacking you. This takes practice, and it requires a great deal of energy. If there is enough space to the outside of an opponent, you can sidestep or use triangular footwork to move to his outside. If you're cornered by multiple opponents, sprinting through one of them with either a hard and protected (keeping your head down) shove or a striking blast can temporarily get you out of the corner. Is there a doorway or other tight space nearby? If it all possible, assuming you can't simply escape, sprint to a place where there is a narrow space between yourself and your opponents, so that they must enter through it and you can fight them one-on-one as they attempt to. This requires practice. If you want to have even the slightest chance of beating multiple opponents, you must add multiple opponent drills to your training.

Certain techniques work better with certain types of footwork. Techniques that require you to step straight into an opponent may not be the best initial techniques to use in a multiple opponent scenario. An eye strike or groin slap works very well with triangular, "counter offensive" footwork, allowing you to attack while simultaneously moving to the outside. Some techniques can be modified to work this way. For example, a boxing cross (done with a palm in self defense, to minimize the chance of a broken hand) is often trained stepping straight in, but can also be used effectively with triangular footwork.

The use of weapons can tremendously add to your chance of success. Using pepper spray or even a bright tactical flashlight (at night) in addition to strategic positioning will make dealing with multiple opponents much easier. But still not easy! If you don't have a projectile weapon, a long range weapon (stick, machete, etc.), which allows you to do damage from a greater distance, will work better than a close range weapon (knife, palm stick, etc.).

5.4.6 Weapons
The mechanics of weapon use and defense is beyond the scope of this book. It will be covered in the next book in this series, but should be mentioned here in terms of training. *If you want to be able to physically defend yourself, you must train to use and defend against weapons.* In my view, fundamental unarmed skills come first. Even when weapons are involved, striking and grappling will very often still occur. Unarmed skills are the base. But you must train defending against modern weapons, and in order to effectively do that, you'll have to learn to use them. You need to be able to use and defend against blunt and sharp weapons of various lengths, and projectile weapons (pepper spray, guns, throwing objects, etc.). If your training does not include weapon use and defense, you're leaving out the *majority* of possible self defense scenarios.

5.5 Conditioned And Default Responses

A *conditioned response* is an automatic reaction to a stimulus, one that is done without thought. Some reactions seem to be genetically programmed, such as quickly pulling a hand away from an object we touch that is dangerously hot. Other reactions require conditioning, or training, in order to ingrain them.

A default response is a particular, purposefully chosen response to a particular stimulus or range of stimuli. Ideally, for self defense a chosen default response has a high probability of success in the widest possible range. A default response that is only effective against a narrow range of stimuli, for example a particular blocking technique that only works against a particular punch, thrown at a particular location, and executed toward a particular part of the opponent's arm, will only succeed in a very specific scenario. In self defense, a practitioner will not know which attack an opponent will launch, how he will launch it, exactly what angle it will come in on, exactly what the target will be, etc. Therefore, an effective default response that covers the widest possible range of attacks will provide the greatest chance of success.

A default response can be conditioned so that it becomes a conditioned response. An effective, wide ranging, conditioned default response is one of the most important, functional self defense tools there is.

Many martial art and self defense systems have a great variety of offensive and defensive techniques. There are multitudes of blocks and defensive techniques for the inside of lead hand straight punches, for the outside of rear hand straight punches, for the inside of a lead hand hook, and so on. Some systems have multiple different counters for backhand attacks depending on how the hand is formed, a hammer fist vs. a backfist vs. a knifehand for example. While it's ok to practice a variety of techniques, assuming they're all functional and effective, *trying* to match a particular and specific defensive technique to a particular and specific offensive technique, at full speed and power, against a random attack from an uncooperative opponent, where the initial technique is likely to be one in a continuous combination attack, is highly unlikely to succeed in reality.

Highly skilled martial artists *can* successfully match particular defense techniques to particular attacks. It happens all the time in both sparring and fighting. But the probability of success decreases as the element of surprise increases. The probability of success when applying a wide ranging conditioned default response is far, far greater.

Imagine a scenario where you're approached by a man who asks you a nonthreatening question. All of a sudden, he throws a punch at you. Was it a perfect jab? Was it a perfect cross? Was it a perfect hook? Which foot did the man have forward? If you don't want to get nailed by the attack, you'll need to do something in a fraction of a second. Would it be easier to identify exactly which punch the man threw, how he threw it, and where he threw it, and choose a block that specifically matches that punch, or would it be easier to quickly respond with a one-size-fits-all default response that works against *all* punching attacks? The answer should be obvious.

A significant portion of your training should be spent on conditioning high probability default responses to various scenarios. In Chapter 7, I'll cover the *Fundamental Five*, a framework of five default responses and follow ups to five different situations. The key to conditioning these default responses is to train them over and over and over again, with full speed and power, using a combination of cooperative partner training, random flowing, and sparring.

5.6 Increasing Skills And Qualities

Functional training will increase a practitioner's speed, power, accuracy, and ability to manipulate and control distance and timing. It's important to realize how these qualities are interrelated, as making use of all five together will maximize skill in self defense, and can make a small and relatively week practitioner seem incredibly fast and powerful. When a large, fast, and strong practitioner utilizes all of these qualities well, he or she will seem super human.

When most people think about speed, the first thing that comes to mind is getting from point A to point B faster. However, speed is as much a function of distance and timing as the actual speed of motion. With good timing, a technique done at moderate speed can seem lightning fast to the receiver. And a very fast technique done at too great a distance can look slow and easy to see coming.

Timing is also very much dependent on distance. Good timing can involve nailing an opponent just as the distance is closing, or moving just out of range to avoid an attack.

While power does depend on strength to some degree, speed, timing, accuracy, and distance also play a big part. The speed of a technique can significantly increase power. The accuracy, or exactly where the technique is applied, can significantly increase the damage that is done. If distance is too close or too great for a given technique, power can be greatly diminished. If an opponent is moving toward you, timing a strike to collide with his mass can multiply the power, but if the timing is poor and an opponent is moving away, a powerful strike can have nearly no impact at all.

A slow technique, due to speed, timing, and/or distance, may fail to accurately hit the intended target due to the opponent having time to move or block.

Below, I'll break down various components of each skill or quality, and explain how to increase them through functional training. But keep in mind that they are all interrelated.

5.6.1 Speed
Speed in Motion: Part of speed is the time it takes to get from point A to point B, and the faster you can move, the better. The best way to increase your speed in motion is to push your limits in order to increase them. Repetition is essential here, and in order to train single techniques with a large number of repetitions, solo or cooperative partner training is ideal. Sparring and random flowing are generally less effective to train this component of speed due to their random nature, which makes them less consistent and harder to do safely while pushing your limits.

Drill: Pick a single technique or combination, and do it over and over again as fast as you possibly can, with the goal of moving even faster each time.

59

Reaction Time: Reaction time, which is the time it takes to act in response to a stimulus, is another element of speed. Cooperative and repetitive training can help to ingrain unconscious reactions, which will always beat conscious reactions, but sparring and random flowing are also important here. Training with an uncooperative partner will give practitioners the ability to adapt to the unexpected, which is another element of reaction time, and thus speed.

> ***Drill #1:*** Pick a single defensive technique, and drill it over and over again in response to your partner's attack. Have the attacker vary the time between attacks, so there is no predictable rhythm. For example, sometimes the attacker may wait 3 seconds before repeating the attack, sometimes 5 seconds, and sometimes he may immediately attack again.
>
> ***Drill #2:*** Sparring. Any form of sparring will help to increase reaction speed.

5.6.2 Timing

Timing is closely related to speed, and in some regards, inseparable. Timing requires speed to ensure that impact is made at the desired moment. And, perceived speed is very much a function of optimal timing. There are three major segmentations relative to an attack:

1. Attack First: Relative to an opponent's attack, in this case, you attack first or *before* the moment of his physical attack. This can include attacking as the opponent sets up to attack, for example, as he raises his hands or makes a threat. To maximize the effectiveness of your attack, you should attempt to attack when and where it is not expected. Attacking an opponent from behind will ensure your attack will land. Attacking from close range, where you do not have to step or lean forward, especially if you can avoid telegraphing the attack with any physical or visual preparation, will make successfully landing the attack a near certainty.

If you cannot attack in such a way that your opponent will not see it coming, you should aim to make your attack as difficult as possible to counter. Executing from a position that makes it difficult to defend against in time and/or trapping/grabbing/controlling one or more of his limbs to stop him from countering the attack, are good examples. This applies to both striking and grappling attacks.

Distance and position really matter here. If you time your attack to land before your opponent attacks, but you begin from a position that both allows him to see it coming and to react to it, you may be putting yourself at a disadvantage. You will be mentally committed to the attack, your opponent will see it coming, and he will have the time to intercept it with an attack of his own. Again, the key to timing your attack first is to do it so that your opponent either doesn't see it coming, or is in a position that makes it very difficult to defend against. Your attack should land like a speeding freight train coming out of nowhere, seemingly materializing a fraction of a inch in front of your opponent and hitting him so fast that he has no clue what hit him.

2. Intercept: An interception is timed so that your attack lands *during* your opponent's attack. The advantage of the interception is that your opponent's mind and body will be momentarily occupied with his attack. In the case of striking, he'll either be moving or shifting toward you, and depending on the counter technique you choose, his motion toward you can magnify the power of your counter.

The key to effectively timing an interception is to attack on your opponent's *motion of convergence*, rather than waiting for or focusing on a particular technique. Obviously, this requires you to see that motion, so you can see your opponent coming. And that requires you to have enough distance, so that your opponent needs to step or lean toward you in order to reach you. Additionally, in order to avoid focusing on a particular technique, your counter must work against a broad range of attacks. If your counter is dependent upon a very specific type of attack, it will be significantly harder to successfully apply, since you'll first have to choose the counter to match the attack. For example, a sidekick to your opponent's knee, as he steps toward you, can land regardless of which punch or kick he attempts to throw. In the technical chapters of this book, I'll highlight techniques and ways of using them that will allow you to counter against a broad range of attacks.

Intercepting an opponent's attack right as he begins to execute it will make you seem much faster than you physically are. One instant your opponent will be preparing to attack you, and the next instant you will have attacked him, before he was able to land his attack. It will seem as though you were able to attack twice as fast as your opponent. In reality, you'll simply have attacked on his motion toward you rather than waiting for his particular attack, allowing him to do the work for you, without realizing it. His motion toward you will also serve to speed up your attack, as his speed toward you will be added to the speed of your own attack. When your opponent is stepping into you, you can reach him twice as fast as if he were standing still and you were advancing.

3. Block and Counter: The block and counter, a sequence where you first block an attack and *then* counter, is one of the most common attack timings trained in traditional martial arts. It's also the least effective, and something you should avoid at all costs. Blocking an attack before countering does nothing to stop your opponent from continuing his attack. If he attacks on the first beat and you block on that beat, there is nothing to stop him from continuing with a second technique on the second beat. With a "block then counter" mindset against an opponent who attacks in combination, you will never get the chance to counter. Not only will you be repeatedly stuck in the blocking phase, but in the chaos of a fight or self defense situation, his attacks will begin to get through your defenses and land. As he advances, his attacks will become too fast and too close for you to effectively defend against.

It is possible that you'll find yourself in a position in which you block without attacking. Your opponent may have unexpectedly attacked first, when you were unable to intercept. If or when this is the case, rather than remaining in a "block then counter" mindset, you should switch to an interception.

What is the difference between "block then counter" and "block then intercept"? The interception relies on position and/or cover to avoid incoming attacks. Blocking does not. In many traditional martial arts and self defense classes, practitioners will learn to stand directly in front of an opponent and block incoming attacks, waiting for the opportunity to counter. Again, if the attacks keep coming, the practitioner will be overwhelmed and eventually struck. If you find yourself blocking an attack, you should immediately switch to the attack/intercept mindset, attacking into the attack while simultaneously moving to a safe/covered position through a combination of distance, position, and physical cover.

The *Covered Blast* concept detailed in the previous chapter makes the value of attacking and intercepting, and the problems with blocking and then countering, obvious. Using the *Covered Blast* in conjunction with timing should allow you to nail your opponent before he even realizes your attack is coming.

> ***Drill #1:*** One practitioner takes the role of attacker, and attempts to successfully attack. The other practitioner takes the role of defender, and attempts to intercept the attack. The attacker should attempt to minimize the defender's ability to intercept by using distance, position, angles of attack, and strategies from the *Covered Blast*.
>
> ***Drill #2:*** Have your partner attack you with a combination attack, where you can only use a defensive technique (block or evasion) against the first move. Then, apply an interception against the successive moves in the combination attack. This drill will help ensure you attack your opponent even when you find yourself surprised and in trouble.

5.6.3 Distance & Position

The ability to manipulate distance and position are essential for the use of the *Covered Blast*. By controlling the distance and relative position between yourself and an opponent, you can maximize your options while minimizing your opponent's. An instructor once told me, "distance is time". The more distance you have, the more time you have. The less distance you have, the less time you have. But distance is also more than time. Combined with position, it dictates what you can and can't do, what options you have, and what options your opponent has. In order to manipulate distance and position in a meaningful way, you need to understand them, and more importantly, to feel them. Feeling only comes through practice. But an intellectual understanding of distance and position can help decrease the time it takes to learn to use them effectively. Knowing where you want to go makes getting there faster.

The best categorical breakdown of distance I've seen is by the *Dog Brothers*, divided into seven "ranges". Here are the seven ranges, along with my descriptions:

1. Before Contact: The *before contact* range is the range at which contact is not possible, even with weapons. If two fighters are holding long staves or swords, the *before contact* range is far enough apart so that even with both fighters extending their weapons fully, the tips cannot touch. Because contact cannot be made, it may seem that this range is unimportant or that little happens here. However, the outcome of a "fight" is largely determined by what happens before contact.

The relative distance and position of fighters determines how and when they can attack, which targets are open and from which angles. It determines where you can attack, and what you need to cover. With or without weapons, *before contact* is where you establish dominance over your opponent, where you set up your attack. *Pre-positioning* takes place in the *before contact* range, and the *covered entry* begins there. Without an understanding of distance and position, without the ability to manipulate them, a *covered entry* is nearly impossible.

2. Weapon Contact: The *weapon contact* range is the range in which two fighters can make their weapons clash, but where they cannot reach each other's bodies with the weapons. This range is obviously wider where longer weapons are involved, and very narrow in unarmed fighting (where only the limbs are considered weapons). In fighting with long weapons, *weapon contact* is a bridge between *before contact* and where damage is done. For example, a practitioner can knock an opponent's weapon aside to create a path for an attack or fake to draw an opponent's weapon to a useless position. In unarmed fighting, the possibility of trapping exists here, grabbing, jerking, pulling, or smacking an opponent's limbs (weapons) into a useless position, to create the opportunity for an attack to land successfully.

The difficulty in making use of the *weapon contact* range is the speed at which fighters converge. *Weapon contact* is generally moved through in a fraction of a second. There is very little time between the distance at which two fighter's arms can touch, and the distance at which a punch can land. VERY little. However, that doesn't make the *weapon contact* range less important. By controlling your opponent's weapons, even if they are his limbs, you control his options. **The key to making use of the *weapon contact* range is strategic entry from *before contact*.** This is what the *Covered Blast* is all about: A strategic and purposeful covered entry from *before contact*, through the *weapon contact* range, where you gain control of your opponent through the use of distance, position, cover, striking, trapping, blocking, and physical controls. These first two ranges, which are neglected to the point of being invisible to many traditional martial artists today, are possibly the most important ranges of all in determining who wins and who loses in a fight or self defense situation.

3. Long Range: In unarmed fighting, *long range* is the range at which practitioners can reach each other with kicks, but not with punches. In stick or sword fighting, it is the range at which opponents can cut each other's limbs, but not reach the body.

4. Mid Range: In unarmed fighting, *mid range* is punching range, where fighters can hit each other with fully extended punches, but not yet with knees or elbows. In stick or sword fighting, *mid range* is where sticks and swords can reach heads and bodies. This is the range where action is fast and furious. You're either nailing your opponent here, or you're getting nailed by your opponent.

5. Close Range: *Close range* is where fighters can hit each other with knees and elbows. However, in the seven ranges classification, it is unattached fighting, where practitioners are striking but not grappling, despite the fact that grappling can and likely will happen at this range. With stick and sword fighting, it is possible for fighters to strike each other with the butts of their weapons.

6. Clinch: This is *close range*, but with stand-up grabbing/grappling/wrestling involved. Unless a fight begins at *close range* and immediately ends with a knock out blow, *close range* will very quickly move to *clinch*. People naturally grab each other when they are close, and despite practitioners of striking based systems wanting to believe otherwise, if a fight last more than a few seconds, a *clinch* will be extremely likely. The *clinch* is also where maximum control in stand up fighting can occur. If you control your opponent in the clinch, the fight is yours to win or lose.

7. Ground: *Ground* is the last of the seven ranges. As the name implies, it refers to being on the ground, and includes wrestling and striking. The *ground* range is vast. There is an incredible variety of positions, escapes, and submissions in ground fighting. Once a fight goes to the *clinch*, *ground* is likely to quickly follow for at least one of the participants. While fighting on the ground is not ideal in self defense, as the surface of the ground may cause injury, and being tied up with an opponent on the ground provides a great opportunity for his friends or partners to beat you, it is essential to have fundamental skills in ground fighting. Learning ground fighting will not only ensure you can handle yourself or escape if a fight or self defense situation ends up on the ground, but will also teach you to better avoid going there in the first place.

> *Drill:* Train various ranges and techniques against others. For example, one practitioner attempts to stay in *long* and *mid range*, while the other attempts to enter to the *clinch*. One practitioner can only use striking, while the other can only use grappling. This training will help make it easier to see and feel the ranges, by isolating the ranges and methods of attack and defense.

5.6.4 Power

Power is a function of a variety of factors, including speed, mass, strength, body mechanics/structure, leverage, and timing. The effect of power is also dependant upon the target. A finger jab to the eye will feel very powerful to the receiver even if executed without much force, whereas a punch in the chest (not recommended) will require a great deal of power to have a substantial effect.

Speed: I've written about speed earlier in this chapter. The faster you move, the more power a technique will have, assuming you don't move so fast as to sacrifice your body mechanics and structure. To maximize power, you should aim to attack as fast as possible.

Mass: Mass is another factor that has great impact on power. If a feather moving at a few meters per second hits you, it will feel like nothing. But if a train moving at the same speed hits you, it will kill you. Mass matters. While there is little you can do to substantially increase your mass, at least in a healthy way, there is a lot you can do to maximize the *use* of your mass when applying a technique. Most beginners punch only with their arm, for example, whereas more advanced practitioners punch with their entire body behind the blow. Applying a joint lock is similar. Whatever technique you're practicing, slow down and try to feel all of your mass behind the technique. If you're not maximizing the use of your mass, doing so can increase your power by a very significant amount.

Strength: The stronger you are, all other things being equal, the more powerful you will be. In the last chapter of this book I'll recommend weight training exercises that will make you stronger. If you're not already training regularly and/or working out, there is a lot you can do to increase your strength in order to increase your power.

Structure: Body mechanics and structure are more important than many people realize, and contribute a great deal to perceived power. If you hold a pencil with two hands, it's easy to snap it in half. But if you stand a pencil up on a table, eraser down, and press with two hands as hard as you can against the tip, it will likely go through your hand. Comparable differences exists in self defense techniques, with poor and good structure and alignment.

64

The bones of your arms and legs are strong even at their weakest points. In their strongest positions and orientations, they are amazingly solid. The default takedown defense I teach provides a great example of the power inherent in good structure.

In the image above I'm using my left arm to stop my opponent from entering and grabbing me. Notice the alignment of the bone in my upper arm with respect to my opponent. As he rushes in, I drop my elbow into his path so that the only way he can get closer to me is to crush the bone in my upper arm. With the structural alignment of my arm, there is no way that's going to happen. At best, my opponent will move me backward. This takedown defense requires very little strength. A small woman can use it against a very large and strong man. The harder the attacker rushes in, the more powerful the defender will feel to him, as he slams into a solid structure based on bone alignment rather than muscular strength.

There are subtle uses of structure in a great variety of techniques, from punching to wrestling, that make a practitioner feel incredibly powerful or strong to the receiver, based primarily on body mechanics and alignment instead of muscular strength.

Leverage: Leverage is another very important factor that contributes to perceived power, especially in grappling. As a simple example, if an opponent has your wrist in one hand and has his other hand just behind your elbow, it can be easy for him to break your arm by hyper extending it. But the further he moves his hand away from your elbow, either up or down your arm, the less leverage he has to break it. Leverage cuts both ways. When applying a technique, you should aim to maximize the effect of leverage in order to maximize power. When defending against a technique, taking away the leverage your opponent has can neutralize his attack. Often, a very small shift or movement can take away leverage, and the effect can seem like magic to someone who doesn't realize what you're doing. Your opponent will feel powerless, and if you can maintain superior leverage, you will feel extremely powerful.

Timing: Good timing can magnify power. If an opponent is moving toward you when you hit him, the power of your strike will include the force of your strike plus the force of his forward movement. Timing a joint manipulation with your opponent's movement will add to the power of your technique in a similar fashion. And, timing a technique to coincide with an opponent's exertion in the same direction will also make it much harder for him to resist the technique.

Drill #1: Although speed is a factor that will increase power, try practicing techniques at a slower speed and pay close attention to how you use your mass, body mechanics, structure, leverage, and timing. You should be able to feel the use of your entire body, along with the best alignment of your bones. Tell your opponent to move around as you attempt to apply various joint manipulations, and notice how you can time your techniques *with* his movements instead of against them.

Drill #2: Let your partner get you in a bad position, just before a joint lock or throw, and try to make very small adjustments that negate his mechanical advantage. Feel where you can move in order to take away his power. Taking away an opponent's power can be as effective as increasing yours.

Drill #3: Practice your striking techniques as hard and fast as you can against a heavy bag, or with a partner holding striking pads. There is no better way to increase the power of your strikes than to practice them with full power.

Drill #4: Wrestle. Clinch and ground grappling will teach you everything you need to know about structure, leverage, and timing.

5.6.5 Accuracy

Accuracy can have a tremendous impact on the effect of power. Striking an opponent in an area of the body that isn't particularly vulnerable is incomparable to striking an area that can easily be damaged. Applying pressure to the wrong part of an opponent's body in an attempt to do a joint manipulation will make the difference between success and failure.

Accuracy requires knowing where and how to apply a technique *and* being able to do it, and that takes practice. Although you will increase your accuracy through many training methods that don't specifically focus on it, it is wise to make it the focus of some training methods or sessions.

Drill #1: Have your partner hold a focus mitt and move it around to make it harder for you to strike. At first, he may simply move the target to different places, stopping long enough for you to hit it, but gradually, have him move it more and more.

Drill #2: Choose a target or two on your opponent's body, and engage in limited sparring where you only attempt to hit those precise targets.

Drill #3: Eye strikes. Have your partner put on safety goggles and boxing gloves. His goal is to punch you, yours is to only hit him in the eye with finger jabs to the eye.

Take-Aways

- Every training method has strengths and weaknesses.
- Use a variety of methods to maximize strengths and to minimize weaknesses.
- You ***must*** train against completely uncooperative partners in order to learn how to fight.
- Uncooperativeness is more than just resistance, it is also fighting back.
- The *MMA Base* is an ideal base from which to learn to deal with striking and wrestling, the fundamental ways in which people fight.
- You must go beyond the *MMA Base* in order to maximize technical advantages and learn to deal with the reality of self defense situations.
- Default responses to general classes of attacks are important for self defense.

Chapter 6
The MMA Base

The MMA Base

The *MMA Base* consists of fundamental techniques and training methods from the systems that make up what is commonly known as *mixed martial arts*. Training in the *MMA Base* is crucial. If you don't know how to kick, punch, knee, elbow, and wrestle, you can't expect to be able to defend against an attacker who is using those techniques against you. The techniques you'll find in the *MMA Base* are the most common techniques people use to attack.

In addition to techniques, the *MMA Base* is also a *delivery system*. It involves practical, efficient, and effective footwork from a grounded but mobile stance, with the legs, arms, and body oriented in a way that allows for both offensive and defensive techniques to be quickly employed.

Many traditional martial arts have alternative bases or delivery systems. However, more often than not, these delivery systems are extremely ineffective. They generally focus more on stances rather than footwork, leading practitioners to be unprepared for the true dynamic nature of a fight. People move when they fight. They move all over the place, and a focus on stances rather than dynamic footwork does not prepare practitioners for real fighting. A large number of traditional martial arts also have practitioners put their hands on their hips, rather than in front of their body, leaving practitioners overly exposed to attack, and too slow to launch an effective and quick offense.

The *MMA Base* includes boxing, Thai boxing, wrestling, and Brazilian jiu jitsu. In all of these systems, the primary training method is sparring. Practitioners who train in the *MMA Base* will very quickly learn to punch and defend against punches, to kick and defend against kicks, and to wrestle. These are fundamental techniques of fighting, and training in the *MMA Base* is *the* best way to learn them.

However, the *MMA Base* is not enough for self defense. Modifications and additions do need to be made to maximize effectiveness in self defense. But, it is the best starting point for training. Practitioners will use the foundation it provides for all fighting, and should also come back to the base training systems regularly.

This chapter will cover fundamental techniques and training methods from the *MMA Base*. It should be the starting point for anyone interested in physical self defense.

6.1 Footwork

The better you are at footwork, the better you will be at all of your standing techniques. Footwork gets you in the optimal position to attack, it adds power to your attacks, and enables your defense. Footwork is the starting point for all techniques, and every technique you do should include some sort of footwork. Consider that when you attempt to strike an opponent, he will move. He will either move because you hit him, or he will move in order to avoid the strike. When your opponent attempts to strike you, you should move to counter or to improve your position.

Footwork is also fairly simple in theory. But don't let that make you think it's less important. Footwork exercises can be a great warm up, and you can and should do training exercises where your partner can use any attack and you use only footwork to avoid his attacks. Try using your footwork to get you just outside of your opponent's attack, where you can simultaneously counter, and also to jam your opponent's attack while simultaneously countering.

6.1.1 Cross Footwork

Cross footwork involves simple forward, backward, left, and right movements (on the lines of a "+" sign), where you first move the foot closest to the direction you want to move in. So if you want to move forward, you move forward with your front foot first, and if you want to move to the right, you move your right foot first.

Cross footwork can be done with either a *step and slide* or a *push shuffle*. With the *step and slide*, you first step with the foot that's closest to the direction you want to move in, and then once that foot has landed, you slide your other foot in the same direction, to get back to a grounded and balanced position. If you want to move forward, you simply step forward with your lead leg, and then move your rear foot forward after your front foot has landed. With the *push shuffle*, your first movement is a drive off the foot opposite the direction you want to move in. So if you want to move forward with a *push shuffle*, you push hard off your back foot, in order to "shuffle" or propel yourself forward, stepping with the front foot, and then bringing the rear foot up to a grounded/balanced position. The *step and slide* and the *push shuffle* look about the same in pictures, since the feet move in the same directions and in the same order. But in practice, the *step and slide* is a slower, more relaxed way to move, while the *push shuffle* is a faster, more powerful way to move. Although you can practice both, in self defense I would focus more on the push shuffle.

Note: Nearly all beginners step off with the initial foot and then bring their other foot too close to the initial foot, narrowing their base and weakening their balance. In the following pictures, pay attention to how I maintain my base after stepping in any direction. Another common mistake, on a right cross step, for example, is to step with the right foot and then bring the left foot directly in line with it, or even past it, so that the feet are "crossed". Again, pay close attention to maintaining a stable base position after each step!

The cross footwork begins from a stable and balanced base position. **After each step, this base position must be returned to!**

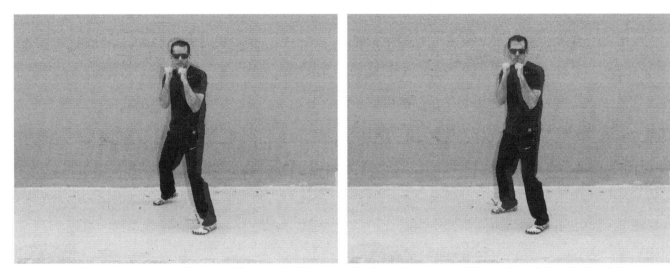

The images above demonstrate the forward step and slide. First the front foot is moved forward, and then the back foot is moved up to the base.

The images above demonstrate the backward step and slide. First the back foot is moved backward, and then the front foot is moved back to the base.

Here you see the left step and slide. First, the left foot is moved to the left, and then the right foot is moved to the base position.

Above is the right step and slide. First the right foot is moved to the right, and then the left foot is moved to the base position.

Here you see the forward push shuffle being used in conjunction with a right boxing cross.

Above, gray shirt uses the forward push shuffle to advance with a boxing jab, and blue shirt uses a backward push shuffle to avoid the jab.

6.1.2 Triangular Footwork

Just as *cross footwork* utilizes the directions of a "+" sign, *triangular footwork* utilizes the directions of an "X". When you combine the directions used in cross footwork and triangular footwork, you have eight directions: forward, backward, left, right, forward right diagonal, forward left diagonal, backward right diagonal, and backward left diagonal.

Triangular footwork comes primarily from Filipino martial arts, and is not typically a part of MMA training. However, I include it in the *MMA Base* because it is extremely effective, can be used with most techniques, and should be a part of your footwork base. *Cross footwork* either moves you directly into or away from your opponent, but *triangular footwork*, particularly the forward variety, can move you both away from and into your opponent. It allows you to intercept an attack or counter attack from a superior position and with a great deal of power.

Here is a demonstration of *triangular footwork*:

In the example above you see right and left forward triangular steps from a neutral position.

Here you see right and left backward triangular steps from a neutral position.

Forward triangular footwork used in conjunction with a groin slap attack.

Forward triangular footwork used in conjunction with an eye strike attack.

First, blue shirt uses a right step and slide to attack gray shirt with a jab. Gray shirt blocks the jab and counters with a cross, and blue shirt uses a short, forward triangle step to get to the outside of gray shirt, to a superior position from which to counter. Ideally, blue shirt would simultaneously counter, but this example serves to demonstrate the use of the triangle step in the context of boxing.

6.1.3 Pendulum Step

The *pendulum step* is the third fundamental type of footwork used in the *MMA Base*. Its use is fairly limited to lead leg kicking, particularly groin kicks. Here is the *pendulum step*:

The rear foot "jumps" or quickly slides up to replace the front foot, and the front foot rises up. The return is the opposite:

On the way back, the front foot comes down to replace the rear foot, and the rear foot returns to its original position.

In the images above you see the pendulum step being used to deliver a groin kick.

6.2 Boxing

Boxing is the perfect stand-up, unarmed system to learn to punch and defend against punches. The base/delivery system is functional and dynamic, and the focus is on experience in sparring and dealing with an uncooperative opponent who is trying to take you out. In self defense, we will modify the punching techniques to use the open hand when striking to the head. But for the *MMA Base* and in the boxing phase of training, closed fists with gloves (for hand and face protection) make sense. The vast majority of people punch with closed fists, which is another reason why practicing with punches is a good thing, to gain familiarity with the most common type of striking attack.

All of the techniques demonstrated here should be trained with a partner using the *I Method*, as described in the previous chapter on training. First, isolate each technique in a cooperative environment, add random flowing with back and forth offense and defense, and then add additional techniques one by one to the mix, as you progress to sparring.

Many people with no fighting experience naturally feel afraid to begin boxing. But no one should be afraid or worried about safe training with a logical progression. Speed and intensity should only be increased as practitioners become comfortable in doing so. Here are the fundamental techniques of boxing:

6.2.1 The Jab

This is the boxing jab, always thrown with the lead hand. Notice the forward motion used to add power to the jab, the raised rear hand, and lowered chin.

The jab is the most common punch thrown in boxing. It's always thrown with the lead hand. So if your left foot is forward, the jab is thrown with your left hand. If your right foot is forward, the jab is thrown with your right hand. Boxers typically pick one lead leg and stick with it. For functional self defense, you should train to box with both a left and a right lead. The jab should be thrown quickly, and your hand must be quickly returned to the starting/base position along the same path it covered going out.

The jab should be practiced with all types of *cross footwork*. Practice it stepping forward, backward, left, right, in place, and ducking. The jab can be used to hurt your opponent, to set him up for other punches, and even defensively. When your opponent is attacking, you can nearly always move and simultaneously jab in order to disrupt his attack.

Your head and chin should always be down when throwing the jab, to keep your face covered and safe.

Notice how my head is lowered in the image above. If my opponent were to simultaneously punch, all he would likely hit is my forehead, or the top of my head. This is very important.

The jab from the front.

The low jab (on the following page) is very similar to the high jab in terms of cover and mechanics. It should not be thrown by bending over at the waist, but by bending the knees or ducking. The low jab makes a great interception against any high attack.

The low jab from two different angles. Notice how the head is still kept down, and the drop is done by squatting rather than bending at the waist.

Here you see blue shirt using the low jab as an interception against both a high left jab and a high right cross.

In the images above you see blue shirt using the jab with sidestepping to simultaneously counter punch against gray shirt's attacks.

6.2.2 The Cross

The images above demonstrate the right cross, a straight punch thrown with the rear hand. Notice how the head is kept down for protection, and the right hip is rotated into the punch.

The cross is a powerful straight punch thrown with the rear hand. In boxing, the cross isn't thrown as frequently as the jab, because despite it being more powerful, it's slower and therefore easier to counter. The cross can be used in isolation, but is more often used in combinations or in counter punching, after a set up of some sort.

Power in the cross can come from a forward step into the target, as with the jab, but it gets even more power due to the rotation of the body. Notice in the images above how the right knee, hip, and shoulder begin in the base position at 45 degrees to the target (front), but at the time of impact are pointed directly at the target. The right side of the body, when throwing a right cross, moves forward and rotates into the target to maximize the mass and power of the punch.

Just like with the jab, your head should be kept down when the cross is thrown, so that if an opponent were to simultaneously punch over your cross, he would hit the top of your head rather than your chin or nose. Your punching hand should retract immediately to the base position as soon as the cross is complete.

On the following page, you see the right cross from another angle:

The low cross is very similar to the high cross. Like the jab, it's thrown by bending the knees instead of the waist. Here is the low cross:

A very low cross, with a full lunge. In most cases, you will not need to go this low, but the example is provided to show how bending is done at the knees and not at the waist.

At left, the low cross is thrown with a slight side step as an interception against a high cross.

6.2.3 The Hook

The left hook. As with the jab and cross, notice how the head is dropped and protected by the lead shoulder. The left hip is rotated into the blow.

The hook is a powerful punch, and like the cross, power is derived from the rotation of the body. More often than not, the hook follows another punch. However, it can certainly be used as the first punch in a combination when the opportunity presents itself. Because the hook is curved and thus has less range than a straight punch, it is most often thrown with the lead hand.

Here is the hook from another angle:

The left hook from the front.

In the images above, notice how the left knee, hip, and shoulder all rotate simultaneously with the hook, and the entire body is used to add mass and power to the hook. Like with all boxing techniques, the head are chin are kept down, so much of the face is protected by the lead shoulder. The rear hand is kept up throughout the motion of the hook.

The hook works particularly well after a low right cross, after a faked jab, or after evading to the opponent's outside, as demonstrated in the following images.

Blue shirt steps to the outside of gray shirt as he covers against a cross, and counters with a hook.

The hook can also be thrown low:

Here you see blue shirt using a low hook after evading gray shirt's cross.

6.2.4 The Uppercut

The right uppercut.

The uppercut is another powerful, curved punch, that often catches opponents unaware due to the path it travels beneath the line of sight. Power in the uppercut comes from rotation, forward movement, and upward drive. When you hit with the uppercut, you should drive down with your feet into the ground to generate upward force.

The uppercut from the front.

The uppercut can target the jaw, solar plexus, or ribs, and works particularly well after a hook, but it can also be thrown as the first punch in a combination when distance and opportunity permit. As with all other punches, notice in the above images that the head is kept low, and the body is rotated to add mass and power to the punch.

Blue shirt evades and covers against gray shirt's cross, and follows with a low hook and a high uppercut.

6.2.5 The Catch

Here you see gray shirt attacking with a jab and blue shirt defending with a catch.

The catch is a simple defense used in boxing that works particularly well against the jab, but can be used against any straight punch. Although we will use the catch in boxing practice, our preference is to simultaneously strike, not to *only* catch/defend. Teaching or practicing the catch and the jab together, for example, allows one practitioner to work his jab while the other works on defense against the jab.

The catch is all about distance and footwork. Notice in the images above how a backward step and slide is done with the catch. Otherwise, gray shirt's punch would blast right through blue shirt's catching hand, and his own hand would hit him in the face.

The catching hand should not reach for the punch. Imagine an invisible shield a few inches from the front of your face. The catching hand should stop at that invisible shield, as if it were pressing up against it, but not extending beyond it. Reaching forward with the catch will provide your opponent with the opportunity to fake the jab and hit you with a lead hand hook. Almost every beginner will reach for the jab with his or her catch. Pay careful attention to avoid this mistake!

A jab-catch drill. Blue shirt steps forward and attacks with a jab. Gray shirt steps backward and defends with a catch. Then it's gray shirt's turn to attack with the jab, and blue shirt's turn to defend with the catch. This can be repeated over and over again. But the timing should be varied so as not to be predictable.

The catch can and should also be done with a simultaneous counter jab. In the images above you see gray shirt attacking with a jab, and blue shirt uses a catch with a simultaneous side step and jab to counter.

6.2.6 The Parry

Blue shirt uses a side step and left parry against gray shirt's cross, and a side step and right parry against the jab. Notice that blue shirt also slips his head to the outside of the punches.

The parry is similar to the catch in that it is a quick and simple technique that can be used against any high straight punch. Like the catch, it can also be used with simultaneous counter punching.

Here you see the parry with simultaneous low counter punches. High counter punches can also be used.

6.2.7 The Shoulder Roll

Gray shirt attacks with a right cross, and blue shirt uses a shoulder roll to evade. Notice that gray shirt has stepped forward and shifted into his punch, punching through blue shirt's former position, but blue shirt is able to evade by only using the shoulder roll.

The shoulder roll is an evasive manoeuvre that involves rotating and shifting the body away from an incoming attack. From a neutral position where the weight, body, and head is centered over both feet, the shoulder roll brings all three over the rear foot/leg. A slight backward step can be used along with it, but to preserve your ability to quickly counterattack, especially from unexpected angles, any backward step should be kept to a minimum.

The shoulder roll can be used to evade any high punch, since you are moving your head out of your opponent's reach, but my preference is to teach it in a drill that involves back and forth shoulder rolls and crosses.

Starting in a neutral position, gray shirt attacks blue shirt with a cross. Blue shirt uses the shoulder roll to evade, and counter attacks with a cross of his own. Gray shirt uses the shoulder roll to evade, and the drill continues. The timing of the attack should be random. Sometimes, the cross should be thrown just after the shoulder roll, and sometimes it should be thrown later, as not to get into a predictable rhythm.

6.2.8 Covers

Blue shirt uses a high cover against gray shirt's hook, and gray shirt uses a low cover against blue shirt's hook.

Covering is a very common defense in boxing, and can work against all types of punches. However, covering is not ideal. Evading a punch completely, ducking, moving your head so it just slips by, or parrying will all allow you to simultaneously counterattack. You should train covers against all punching attacks, but only use them as a last ditch defense. Moving and counter punching is a better option.

The key to making covers work is to keep them tight and close to your body. A cover that is held too far away from your body will give your opponent the opportunity to strike around it, and if he strikes your cover, you may end up getting hit by your own arm.

A cover does not redirect a blow. It simply covers a target so you get hit on the arm rather than getting hit in the face, for example. Obviously, getting hit in the arm is far better than getting hit in the face, but without gloves, covering against a punch can also hurt and/or damage your limbs.

Blue shirt covers against a low jab, and gray shirt covers against an uppercut.

Blue shirt attacks gray shirt by stepping to the outside with a jab, but gray shirt covers the jab and counters with a cross. Blue shirt uses a triangular step with a cover, to get to a better position, and then counterattacks with low and high left hooks. Gray shirt covers the first hook, which leave him exposed to the second. Combining movement with cover gives you more protection against follow up strikes.

6.2.9 Ducking

Blue shirt ducks and counter punches against gray shirt's attacks.

Ducking is an extremely effective way to avoid an opponent's high line attack and to simultaneously counter. It works well in the context of boxing, and even better in self defense, where very few people expect you to drop and simultaneously counter.

When an opponent attacks with a high punch, his lower body will necessarily be exposed. Hitting him hard in the solar plexus or ribs is easy with a well timed duck. Your opponent will be focused on his attack, which will leave him open, and you will have dropped out of his line of site. The same instant you disappear, your opponent is getting hit.

The key to making the duck work is to bend primarily at the knees rather than at the waist. When your opponent steps toward you to attack, you quickly drop and counter attack. Later in this chapter, in the *boxing blast* section, you'll find more examples using the duck.

6.2.10 The Bob and Weave

The bob and weave is like a circular duck, where you begin to duck out to one side of an opponent's attack and circle around to the other side as you rise. A simple duck and counter is quicker. But if you've parried or ducked and countered, and your opponent is still continuing his attack, the bob and weave can make it easier for you to continue your attack without being hit.

Blue shirt parries and sidesteps to avoid gray shirt's jab, but gray shirt keeps coming. Blue shirt uses the bob and weave to get to the outside of his cross and counters with a hook.

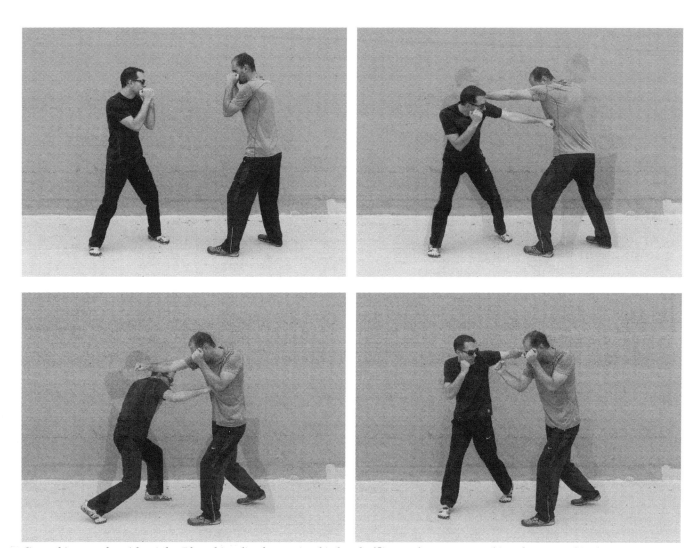

Gray shirt attacks with a jab. Blue shirt slips by moving his head offline and counter punching, but gray shirt keeps coming. Blue shirt uses a bob and weave, hitting gray shirt along the way, and coming up with a left hook.

6.2.11 The Boxing Blast (Alternating Crosses)

In the martial art of *wing chun*, there is an attack called the *straight blast*. It involves blasting your opponent with a well timed, continuous forward pressure barrage of straight punches. Using boxing techniques, a similar type of blast can be used. However, it falls outside of standard boxing, as it requires a constant change of leads. This *boxing blast* consists of alternating crosses, or alternating rear hand punches.

The boxing blast can work extremely well to overwhelm an opponent, either taking him out completely, or causing him to cover and expose other openings you can then exploit. The key to making the boxing blast work, especially against someone with boxing experience, is timing. If you simply launch a blast from a distance, any good boxer will see it coming, will move offline, and nail you with a counter punch.

The boxing blast works best after a set up. The set up may be a jab that causes your opponent to evade or cover, or a counter punch where you hit him once, and then blast him. Regardless of what set up you use, the blast should take your opponent by surprise, and it must be hard, and with continuous forward pressure. However, the alternating crosses in the blast should not be done for more than three punches. Otherwise, your opponent will have time to adapt, move, and counter.

Here are a few examples of the boxing blast, used after a low jab intercept.

Continued on next page...

Gray shirt attacks blue shirt with a jab. Blue shirt intercepts by ducking and hitting gray shirt with a low jab, and then begins the boxing blast. He hits gray shirt with a right cross, steps forward with his right foot and does a left cross, and then steps forward with his left foot and does a right cross. The crosses are timed to land just before the lead foot hits the ground. Gray shirt has covered his face in response to the boxing blast, after being struck by the first cross, which gives blue shirt the opportunity to nail him with an uppercut to the solar plexus and a hook to the jaw. Notice that blue shirt also takes a step into and to the side of gray shirt for the uppercut.

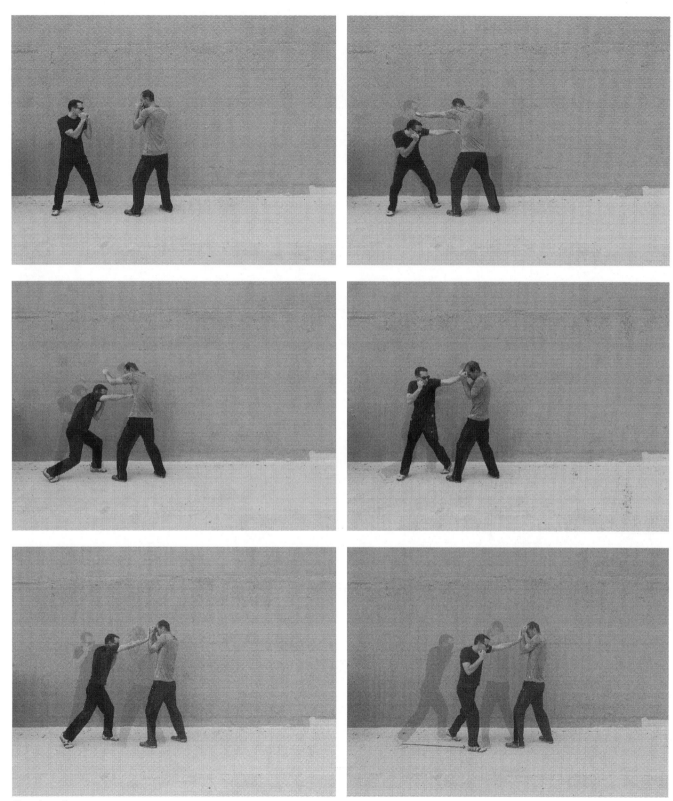

Continued on next page...

Gray shirt attacks blue shirt with a jab, and blue shirt ducks and counter punches (Keep in mind that this defense would work against any high punch gray shirt may have thrown.). Blue shirt hits gray shirt twice in the ribs, with a low jab and a low cross, causing gray shirt to drop his hands, leaving him open for a high left hook. The high hook is followed by the boxing blast. Blue shirt throws a right cross, and then steps forward with his right foot, switching leads and throwing a left cross. As gray shirt covers against the high line attack, blue shirt steps again, switching leads, and nails gray shirt with an uppercut - hook combination.

In the following sections you'll find more examples of the boxing blast, followed up with kicks, knees, and elbows.

6.3 Kick Boxing

While you're less likely to come in contact with a kicking attack in self defense scenarios, adding kicks to your boxing-style training adds a number of powerful and effective weapons to your toolbox. In FSD we tend to keep kicks low, normally below the waist. Occasionally, we use higher kicks in sparring, but for self defense high kicks are low percentage moves that are dangerous to attempt in most situations. In this section, I'll cover some of the most effective kicks from Thai boxing and jeet kune do, along with defenses against them.

6.3.1 The Groin Kick

A simple but effective groin kick, using a pendulum step to advance.

The groin kick is one of my favorite kicks for self defense. It's not trained in MMA systems, as kicks to the groin are illegal in MMA, but I'm including it here because it fits well and is so effective. First, it should be said that the groin kick is not *necessarily* a fight stopper. However, on the couple of occasions where I've used the groin kick myself, my opponent has fallen to the floor. And, a quick YouTube search for "mma groin kick" will result in numerous videos of MMA fighters being taken out with a single accidental groin kick, even while wearing cups. A solid and well placed kick to the groin will likely have a very significant effect, but don't count on it. It's also easy enough to miss.

The fastest way to do a groin kick is to simply launch one from close range. If you're not close enough to land it, a pendulum step (detailed in the footwork section of this chapter) works very well, as does first leading with a jab to occupy your opponent on the high line, as in the following images:

Blue shirt uses a jab followed by a pendulum step to launch a groin kick. Gray shirt uses a knee raise block.

A triangular step to your opponent's outside can also work well:

Blue shirt takes a triangular step to the outside of gray shirt's striking range in order to set up a safe groin kick.

One of the best times to use a groin kick is just as your opponent is stepping forward to attack. His weight will be landing on his lead leg, making it nearly impossible for him to lift his knee to block the kick, or to get his hand down in time to stop it, particularly if he is attempting to attack you with it. Either a sideward *step and slide* or a backward triangular step can work well.

Gray shirt attacks blue shirt with a punch. Just as gray shirt begins to step forward, blue shirt steps off line and fires his kick. Note: The images above aim to demonstrate the footwork and kick separately. However, they should be done as one movement. The kick should hit gray shirt just as his lead leg lands, making it almost impossible for him to block.

The groin kick should not be done as it is taught in most traditional martial arts, as a "snap kick". In many systems, practitioners are taught to bring their knee up first, and then snap the kick out. Although it can be smooth, this necessarily leads to an increase in the distance the foot must travel and the time it takes to land. Instead, the kicking foot should be launched in nearly a straight line, directly to the target, and hitting like a whip. Depending on the situation, the kick may travel straight up, or inward at an angle.

The groin kick may also be done with the rear leg. After a boxing blast or punching combination, your opponent may cover high, leaving his groin open. If your striking attack has ended with your weight on your lead leg, a rear leg groin kick can make sense.

Gray shirt attacks blue shirt with a punch. Blue shirt intercepts with a low jab, but gray shirt keeps coming. Blue shirt uses a bob and weave with a simultaneous low cross, and then steps forward, switching leads and throwing a left cross to drive gray shirt back. As gray shirt covers high, blue shirt has the opportunity to launch a groin kick. His weight is on his lead leg, so he kicks with his rear leg.

6.3.2 The Side Kick

Blue shirt uses a pendulum step to launch a lead leg sidekick into gray shirt's knee.

The side kick is common in most martial arts, and can be an effective weapon in self defense. Due to the physical orientation required for the side kick, the recovery of a kick above the waist is relatively long. A higher side kick will put your side or even your back to your opponent after completion, and for that reason, we generally only use side kicks to the knee in FSD.

The side kick can be used as a *stop kick*, to intercept your opponent's forward motion, and works very well against a wide variety of striking attacks. However, against a much larger opponent, the chance of success will decrease due to the comparatively greater momentum of the larger attacker and the increased difficulty in actually damaging his knee joint.

As an attack, if you're not close enough to simply launch the kick and nail your opponent, pendulum steps and triangular steps can work well. Triangular steps can give you an even better shot at damaging your opponent's knee joint, as they allow you to attack the knee from a more vulnerable angle.

Just like with the groin kick, you should avoid using the side kick the way it is taught in most traditional martial arts, with the knee brought up fully and then launching the kick. You'll find you can get just as much power by quickly bringing your foot to the target in a straight line, and using a stomping action at the moment of impact. The outer edge of your foot should impact your opponent *just* above his knee, stomping through in order to maximize the chance of hyper-extending or damaging the joint.

As gray shirt begins to move forward to attack blue shirt, blue shirt launches a side kick/stop kick, attacking gray shirt's lead knee.

As gray shirt steps forward to attack, blue shirt uses a triangular step with a cover to get to a safe position and avoid the attack. The instant his left foot hits the ground, his right foot nails gray shirt in the knee from a vulnerable angle with gray shirt's weight on his lead leg.

6.3.3 The Thai Kick

The Thai kick to the thigh. Note how blue shirt steps off to his outside and swings his hip and body fully in, to add power to the kick.

The Thai kick is a unique and powerful kick from Thai boxing. Many traditional styles use a roundhouse kick that travels a similar path, but the roundhouse kick uses a snapping or whipping motion. The Thai kick instead slams into an opponent like a baseball bat. The entire body is swung, full force, into the kick.

In Thai boxing and MMA, it is thrown to the inside and outside of both legs, to the ribs, and to the head. In FSD, we primarily use the Thai kick to target the outside of the leg or thigh. If the inside of the leg is open, a groin kick is a better option. In most situations, the ribs are unlikely to be open to kicking, and higher Thai kicks are more likely to be caught. While head kicks can work, they are generally low percentage moves and dangerous to attempt on the street in most circumstances. Kicking the outside of the thigh with a Thai kick can easily drop a person, particularly if he or she has not been exposed to repeated Thai kicks. The aim is to nail your opponent with your shin, and not with your foot. Think about driving the edge of your shin bone into your opponent's muscle.

A Thai kick is a fully committed kick. While the recovery isn't as bad as with a high side kick, it is substantial. Therefore, it is best to use the Thai kick in combination with a punching attack, as demonstrated in the following images:

Blue shirt uses a jab - cross combination to cause gray shirt to cover high. When gray shirt is busy defending against the high line punches, blue shirt nails him in the thigh with a Thai kick.

Another advantage to setting up a Thai kick with punches, particularly high punches, is that they can cause your opponent to cover, obscure his vision, and make it easier for you to land the kick.

Take a look at the images above. After the right cross, most of blue shirt's weight is on his lead (left) leg. Gray shirt has his left leg forward. So the quickest kick is a right Thai kick to the outside of gray shirt's thigh. If gray shirt would have stepped back with his left leg, and had his right foot forward, blue shirt would not have used the Thai kick, but a groin kick. As a rule of thumb, if your weight is on your lead leg and you and your opponent have *matched leads*, a Thai kick is the best option. If your weight is on your lead leg but you and your opponent have unmatched leads, a groin kick makes more sense.

6.3.4 Other Kicks

Various martial arts use a number of additional kicks. However, the majority of those kicks are impractical for self defense, and rarely used in MMA. The groin kick demonstrated in this chapter can be thrown upward or inward. It's a very quick, damaging kick. The Thai kick is thrown inward, with body mechanics that are substantially different from the groin kick. And the side kick allows you to kick from the side. With those three kicks alone, you should be able to effectively kick your opponent from nearly any relative position and do damage if your kick lands.

Kicks that are thrown to the outside, such as a crescent kick, which is common in karate and tae kwan do, have relatively little power and are dangerous to attempt on the street. There are several variations of spinning back kicks, but they are very low percentage techniques that would best be avoided. The only other kick I'd consider adding to the *MMA Base* is the push kick or *teep*, from Thai boxing:

As gray shirt begins to move forward, blue shirt nails him with a push kick or Thai "teep". Notice how blue shirt thrusts his hips forward to add power to the kick.

On the surface, the push kick looks like a "front kick" used in many traditional martial arts. However, it is not a snap kick, and the force of the kick is primarily straight forward, into the opponent, rather than upward. One of the most important components of the push kick is the forward drive of the hips, to blast into the opponent. The problem with the push kick, and the reason I consider it optional, is that it only works well on a similar sized or smaller opponent. Against a larger opponent, the push kick isn't likely to have much effect.

6.3.5 Blocking Kicks

Gray shirt blocks blue shirt's Thai kick with a simple knee raise block.

The best way to deal with an incoming kick is to get out of the way. Kicks can come in with a great deal of power, and even if you do block them, they can hurt, knock you back, and potentially cause damage. If you cannot get out of the way, low kicks are best blocked with a simple knee raise, as demonstrated in the images above and below. You will still be getting kicked, but rather than on a vulnerable target, you will be kicked on your lower leg. To block a kick with the outside of your leg (like a Thai kick, see above), it's best to try to use the muscle on the outside of your lower leg. This won't hurt as much as using your shin bone. If you're blocking a kick with the inside of your lower leg, it's going to hurt. Try turning your knee into the kick in order to hit more with your muscle than bone, or try to direct your knee into the kicker's ankle. This will likely hurt the kicker more than it hurts you.

Some martial arts train blocking low kicks with a low downward sweep of the arm, but there are several problems with this method. It's unlikely your arm will reach down far enough and fast enough to block a leg kick, unlikely that you'll have enough power in your arm to stop the kick, and you'll be opening your head to easy follow-up attacks. For leg and groin kicks, the best bet is to either get out of the way, move your leg out of the way, or use a knee raise block.

Gray shirt blocks a groin kick with a simple knee raise, aiming to hit blue shirt's ankle with his knee.

When you do use a knee raise block, it's very important to keep your hands up. Sometimes it's hard to tell whether a kick is coming in high or low, and if a kick does come higher, you can use your boxing style covers to block it.

Gray shirt thinks blue shirt's kick is coming in low, and brings his knee up to block it. When it goes high instead, he is still ready with a high cover.

Some kicks can be blocked by a downward block with the arm. However, oftentimes moving out of the way without the block would accomplish the same thing. Here are two examples of blocking a push kick with a downward block:

Blue shirt demonstrates an outside downward block and an inside downward block against gray shirt's push kick.

Again, the easiest way to deal with a kick is to avoid it. But if you can't, then a knee raise for low kicks, a downward block for mid level kicks, and covers for high kicks are going to be your best options. If you're up against a kicker, getting inside his kicking range and blasting with punches or establishing a control position will take out his ability to kick. It's always easier to close distance than to maintain an unattached range, which suits the close range fighter.

As for training kicking and kicking defense, you should integrate kicking just like boxing and boxing defense. You can work a single kick in isolation with a single kicking defense, and then add additional kicks. You can also add single or multiple kicks to your boxing base. The end goal is to use all of your boxing and kickboxing techniques in a random environment.

6.4 Knees And Elbows

Knees and elbows are your most powerful strikes. Hitting someone in the face with an elbow can literally be like hitting them in the face with a hammer. There is no padding on your elbow, and no joints to compress and soften the blow as is the case with hand and foot strikes. I once accidentally clipped a student of mine with an elbow in the face. It broke her temple, cheek bone, and eye socket, and required surgery to put a metal plate in her face in place of the shattered bones. A fast elbow with your entire mass behind it can do tremendous damage. Knees are the same. A hard knee in the solar plexus or face can be devastating, as can a knee to the groin or thigh.

As you'll see in the next chapter, my primary aim in physical self defense is to get control of my opponent so I can hammer him with knees and elbows, or apply effective joint manipulations or chokes. In the *MMA Base*, you should add knees and elbows to your sparring progression. However, you will have to keep the intensity lower in order to be safe.

On the following pages are the knee and elbow strikes you should have in your arsenal.

6.4.1 Knees

Blue shirt knees gray shirt in the solar plexus. Notice how blue shirt is grabbing gray shirt behind his neck, and pulling him into the knee strike. Blue shirt also has control of gray shirt's right arm, and has his head down below the grabbing arm to provide cover against a potential punch from gray shirt's left hand.

Blue shirt knees gray shirt in the groin. Again, notice how blue shirt keeps his head down, maintains control of gray shirt's "near" arm, and pulls him into the knee strike.

The most common knee strike, shown in the last four images, travels both upward and forward. The power comes from quickly and strongly driving the knee upward, and simultaneously driving the hips forward and through the target. Different targets will require different degrees of upward and forward force. For example, a knee to the groin will typically be more upward, but still a bit forward, whereas a knee to the solar plexus will have a much greater forward component.

In all four of the previous images, notice how blue shirt has control of gray shirt with his hands or arms, and pulls gray shirt into the knee strikes. At close range, where knees and elbows are possible, you will be within striking range. Therefore, it's extremely important to maintain cover and control in this range. In the previous four images, blue shirt can use his arm, against gray shirt's neck, to drive gray shirt away at any time. And, he can use the same arm as a shield to duck under in case gray shirt throws a punch.

From a similar control position, if blue shirt has access to gray shirt's side, he can also target the thigh with a knee strike, attacking the same area as he would with a Thai kick.

Blue shirt attacks gray shirt with a knee to the solar plexus. In these images, blue shirt uses triangular footwork to get to the outside of gray shirt, control him, and knee him. This "covered entry" can be used as an attack, or as an interception against a punch.

Here, blue shirt has control of gray shirt's head, and pulls his head into a knee strike.

Knee strikes can also be delivered from the high tie-up or "Thai clinch", which will be covered in detail in the next section of this chapter.

If you're close enough to your opponent for him to attempt to knee you, and he does, moving out of the way probably won't be an option. You'll need to block the knee. Here are a few good options:

Gray shirt uses a lead knee raise to block blue shirt's knee strike.

When blue shirt attacks from the other side, gray shirt uses his rear knee to block the strike.

When he cannot use his knee to block, gray shirt uses an elbow strike/block to stop blue shirt's knee.

Again, where gray shirt is unable to use his knee to block the attack, he uses his arms. In the first example he uses both arms to stop a knee to the face, and in the second he uses a single arm to block and pass the knee strike.

6.4.2 Elbows

Blue shirt demonstrates a high horizontal elbow strike against gray shirt. Notice how blue shirt shifts his hips into the elbow strike.

The first fundamental elbow strike is a horizontal strike that follows a motion similar to a boxing hook. The elbow is swung up, around, and into the opponent. On the front of the body, effective targets are the nose, jaw, and solar plexus. On the side of the body, the temple, jaw, and ribs can also be targeted. And on the back of the body, the back of the neck and kidneys are good targets. *Keep in mind that elbow strikes are dangerous, and can potentially kill a person. They should not be used lightly.*

A right horizontal elbow may be followed with a left horizontal elbow, if your opponent is still in range.

Two horizontal elbow strikes are shown in the above images, where blue shirt hits gray shirt in the front of the face with a right elbow, and then in the jaw with a left elbow. Although this right - left elbow combination is trained in many systems, it's unlikely to work exactly as such. If the right elbow misses, then it's possible to use a left elbow. However, it's more likely that gray shirt will either be knocked back by the right elbow, too far for the left elbow to land, or he'll have his hands up, blocking a secondary high elbow strike. A more likely combination is as follows:

Blue shirt hits gray shirt in the face with a left elbow, yanks him into a left knee to the solar plexus, and follows with a right elbow to the temple.

After throwing a horizontal elbow to the face or front of the body, your opponent will most likely have backed up either due to getting hit, or due to having blocked the strike. Immediately after such an elbow, grabbing the back of your opponent's neck with the same hand or arm that executed the elbow, can work very well, as the grab will give you twice the range of the elbow. Yanking your opponent into a knee strike will serve to bring him back into range for another elbow, not to mention the knee strike, and make it harder for him to block due to the quick high-low-high nature of the combination.

A vertical elbow can be used to target the solar plexus or face. Like the basic knee strike, the vertical elbow has both upward and forward force components that vary in degree depending on the target.

Downward elbows can also work in some situations. Above, a downward elbow is used after gray shirt bends over due to a kick to the groin. Notice how blue shirt grabs the back of gray shirt's head to control him and bring him into range.

The key to generating maximum power with any elbow strike is a combination of speed and getting your mass behind the blow. Your elbow is closer and more connected to your center of mass than your fist or foot. By moving your elbow as quickly as possible, staying relaxed, but keeping your mass behind the blow, you'll have an incredibly powerful strike. Aim for speed, and contract your muscles heavily only on and through impact.

Unlike with knee strikes, where your opponent will be likely to have a degree of physical control over you before attacking, it is more often possible to evade an elbow strike. However, in many cases where you cannot evade an elbow, you will have to block. Here are a couple of possible elbow blocks:

The blocking technique above is shown at a greater distance than is realistic for the sake of demonstrating the technique. As blue shirt attacks gray shirt with an elbow, gray shirt grabs the back of blue shirt's neck. The angle of his grab jams blue shirt's elbow, and simultaneously gives him control of blue shirt.

Blue shirt uses boxing style covers to defend against gray shirt's elbow attacks.

6.5 Clinch

The low and high tie ups.

If a fight lasts more than a few seconds, it's highly likely that it will go to the clinch. When two people strongly blast toward each other, it happens naturally, and it happens fast. The clinch can be a place of transition, a bridge between stand up and ground, or between striking and grappling. But it's also a place where with the right skills, you can quickly take out your opponent. The clinch occurs at the optimal range for the most damaging techniques: knees, elbows, chokes, and joint manipulations. And, it's relatively easy to prevent your opponent from hitting you with solid punches in the clinch. If you know how to control your opponent and apply effective techniques here, and if your opponent does not, you win.

In MMA the primary clinch positions come from wrestling and Thai boxing. In this section, I'll cover the two primary positions trained in MMA, the *high tie up* and the *low tie up*, along with a number of transitions, techniques, and counters in each. These positions, and the ability to fight from them, are extremely important. They are very natural, and very common. However, for self defense, I prefer a couple of additional clinch positions that give a practitioner a greater level of control with better and quicker options. I'll cover those in the next chapter, in the section titled *Control Positions*, along with how to get into these positions.

6.5.1 The Low Tie Up

The low tie up (pictured above, left), occurs when two people grab each other in a zone between the waist and shoulders. The standard position, from which both practitioners have equal opportunities, is where each practitioner has one hand grabbing their opponent's back, and the other grabbing their opponent's triceps (as pictured above). The first exercise that should be trained from this standard position is called "pummeling" or "swimming", where each practitioner attempts to get both arms around their partner's back, like in an under-the-arm bear hug or "body lock", but because both practitioners are doing the same thing, they more often simply end up switching sides.

Swimming And The Body Lock

In the second image above, blue shirt attempts to "swim" or thread his left arm underneath gray shirt's right arm. But, gray shirt is doing the same thing on the opposite side. Blue shirt gets his right arm underneath, but gray shirt also gets his left arm underneath. They end up in the same position as they started, but reversed.

If blue shirt can get both arms under gray shirt's arms, he can apply a "body lock", pulling in with both arms and pushing forward with his head. This will easily drive gray shirt to the ground.

If your partner gets you with the body lock, you can use the whizzer to break the hold. To do the whizzer, drop and shift your weight to your far leg, simultaneously turning and wrenching your partner's arm. Be careful in training not to hyper-extend your partner's elbow with the whizzer.

A simple way of getting comfortable with the low tie up is to pummel or swim for position, where both you and your partner attempt to get the body lock. You'll find that most of the time, you'll end up switching positions and neither of you will get it. But when one of you does get the body lock, then the other one can attempt the whizzer. The main point of this limited practice is to get comfortable with the low tie up.

A variation of this exercise involves both practitioners attempting to get a body lock or put the other's back against a wall. This variation will increase your ability to move and control your opponent in the clinch, and to avoid being controlled by him. A little practice here goes a long way. People clinch naturally, but very few have clinch skills. Therefore, training can give you a significant advantage here if your opponent has not trained clinch.

The Arm Drag

The arm drag is an excellent technique that works in a variety of situations. It should be added to your practice in the low tie up, along with a number of follow ups:

Blue shirt slides his left hand down gray shirt's arm and grabs his wrist. He then grabs the back of gray shirt's right arm with his right hand. He pushes gray shirt's hand down and off of his back, and then uses his right arm to pull gray shirt's arm to the other side.

Blue shirt uses the arm drag to pull gray shirt into a choke.

Blue shirt uses the arm drag to pull gray shirt into a bear hug, from which he can easily throw him to the ground.

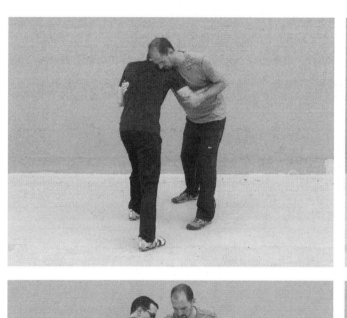 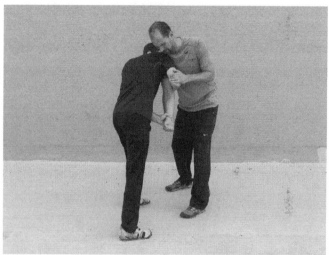

Blue shirt uses the arm drag to get a two-on-one arm control on gray shirt. Notice that blue shirt's left hand is grabbing gray shirt's arm just above his elbow, and his right hand is grabbing gray shirt's wrist. From this position blue shirt can lock or break gray shirt's elbow, and easily move and control him.

To escape from the two-on-one, gray shirt grabs blue shirt's wrist with his left hand, and punches his right hand out as he pulls on blue shirt's wrist. He then uses his free hand to grab and pull blue shirt's arm by, with an arm drag of his own. After the arm drag, gray shirt switches grips and gets the two-on-one.

Once you and your partner have practiced swimming for the body lock, you should add the arm drag to the mix, with the bear hug, choke, and two-on-one follow ups. Then, add the single under hook, demonstrated on the following page:

The Single Underhook

Blue shirt uses his left hand to grab gray shirt's arm at the bend, and pushes it away. He then hooks gray shirt's left shoulder from underneath with his right hand. Blue shirt applies upward pressure with his right arm and forward pressure with his left hand and arm. The resulting position is called the single underhook.

The single underhook (see above) may not look like much, but it's a surprisingly solid position that gives you good control of your opponent. Because your opponent's weight will be on his rear leg, he will not be able to use it to knee you. But you will be able to knee him with your rear leg.

The most common response to a single underhook by an untrained person is to attempt to put you in a head lock with the underhooked arm. Fortunately, this will give you the opportunity for a "duck under", putting your opponent in an even worse position, as seen in the images on the next page.

Gray shirt attempts to put blue shirt in a head lock with his left arm. Blue shirt uses a duck under to get to gray shirt's back. From behind, blue shirt can throw, choke, or strike gray shirt at will. In the images above, blue shirt secures a "harness" on gray shirt, throwing his right arm over gray shirt's shoulder and grabbing it with his left hand. He then pulls gray shirt to the ground.

Single And Double Leg Takedowns

Single and double leg takedowns are also possible from the low tie up. Here is an example of a double leg takedown:

Blue shirt drops down, grabs both of gray shirt's legs, and rises, throwing him to the ground with a double leg takedown.

While single and double leg takedowns are very common in wrestling and in MMA, in FSD we tend to avoid using them since our preference is not to take a fight to the ground, but to remain standing. Although you can obviously use a single or double leg takedown to bring your opponent down while you remain standing, your opponent's counter (good or bad) may end up bringing you to the ground with him. The most important reason to practice these takedowns is to learn how to counter them in case an opponent attempts to use one on you.

Whenever possible, our preference in defending against a single or double leg takedown is the takedown defense demonstrated in the following chapter. However, from a low tie up you may not have the distance or position from which to use it. In that case, a sprawl can be used to smother the takedown attempt.

Gray shirt drops to get a double leg takedown on blue shirt, but blue shirt quickly shoots both legs backward driving his hips and body down and stopping gray shirt from getting the hold required to make the takedown.

Striking In The Low Tie Up

Once you've gotten comfortable wrestling in the low tie up, swimming, going for body locks, arm drags, single underhooks, and takedowns, you should add striking to the mix. It's more difficult than you may think to be successful with punches, as you generally need both hands to control your opponent, and if you give up that control in an attempt to strike, your opponent will be able to quickly gain a superior position from which to apply much more damaging techniques.

The easiest striking techniques to use in the low tie up (without getting to a better control position first) are knee strikes:

The best way to defend against a knee strike is to position your leg and body so you aren't vulnerable to one in the first place, to push or pull your opponent to prevent him from being able to execute a knee, or to block it by putting your knee in the way.

Groin slaps and grabs can also work from the low tie up. However, they can provide your opponent with an opportunity to get an arm drag or to get your back. The best way to prevent this from happening is to hang on to your opponent's testicles and/or pants, and pull them forcefully. This will stop your opponent from being able to drag your arm or get behind it. If your groin slap/grab has injured your opponent, then you can transition to other striking, locking, or choking. If you've missed, you can transition back to the low tie up.

The groin slap/grab demonstrated from matched and unmatched leads.

In the images above, blue shirt uses the groin slap from both matched and unmatched leads. In the first set of images (top), blue shirt could have used a knee strike to the groin. In the second set of images (bottom), blue shirt's rear knee is not positioned to strike gray shirt effectively. In this case, a groin slap/grab is the better option. Generally, when you're unable to knee in the low tie up, you will be able to use a groin slap/grab.

Notice that gray shirt's hand is on blue shirt's groin slapping elbow. The best way to counter the groin slap is for gray shirt to either keep blue shirt's arm tight so he cannot use his hand in such a way, or to pass his arm by as he attempts to groin slap, getting to blue shirt's back.

6.5.2 The High Tie Up

The high tie up involves grabbing the back of an opponent's head or neck. The first exercise to become accustomed to the high tie up and the options from that position is similar to the first exercise from the low tie up:

Blue shirt attempts to thread his left hand inside gray shirt's right arm in order to get both hands on the inside, grabbing gray shirt's neck/head. But, gray shirt is doing the same thing with is left arm, countering blue shirt simultaneously. They both thread their outside hand to the inside, leading to a reversal of positions. In the third image, they are further apart than they would be in reality to better demonstrate the switch in these images.

In the equal high tie up, where each practitioner has one hand on his partner's neck/head and the other grabbing his arm, their position is equal. The goal in pummelling for position is to have both hands grabbing your opponent's head and neck, in order to have full control of your opponent's head.

The key to maximizing your control when you do have both hands on the inside is to torque your hands inward as if you were attempting to scoop his neck toward you. This will put your opponent in an awkward position from which it will be nearly impossible for him to attack. From this position, it will be relatively easy to throw your opponent around by his head, even if he is bigger and stronger.

By stepping back and twisting gray shirt's head from the full control position of the high tie up, blue shirt can easily sling gray shirt around. This can be particularly effective if there is something to throw gray shirt into, or if you follow with knees.

From full control in the high tie up, blue shirt pulls gray shirt into a knee to the face.

If your opponent is able to get both of his hands on the inside in a high tie up, your first priority should be escaping from this inferior position, as you will not have a good base to attack from, but your opponent will. The easiest way to do so is to thread one of your hands back to the inside. But if you're not able to, here are two additional options:

Blue shirt has full control of gray shirt in the high tie up, with both hands on the inside. Gray shirt is unable to thread either of his hands to the inside, so he uses a "face push" to create enough space to either thread a hand in, or to strike blue shirt.

Gray shirt uses a motion similar to a karate-style inward forearm block to break blue shirt's hold on his head/neck. Notice that gray shirt shifts his body into the block to add power.

While having full control of your opponent's head is ideal in the high tie up, you can also attack from a position of equal control. In the following images, blue shirt uses his inside arm to shove gray shirt away and then yank him back into strikes. In order to shove gray shirt away blue shirt smacks him with the inside of his forearm.

Blue shirt shoves gray shirt out with his right arm and yanks him into a knee, grabbing the back of gray shirt's neck with both hands. He then shoves gray shirt out again, and yanks him into an elbow strike.

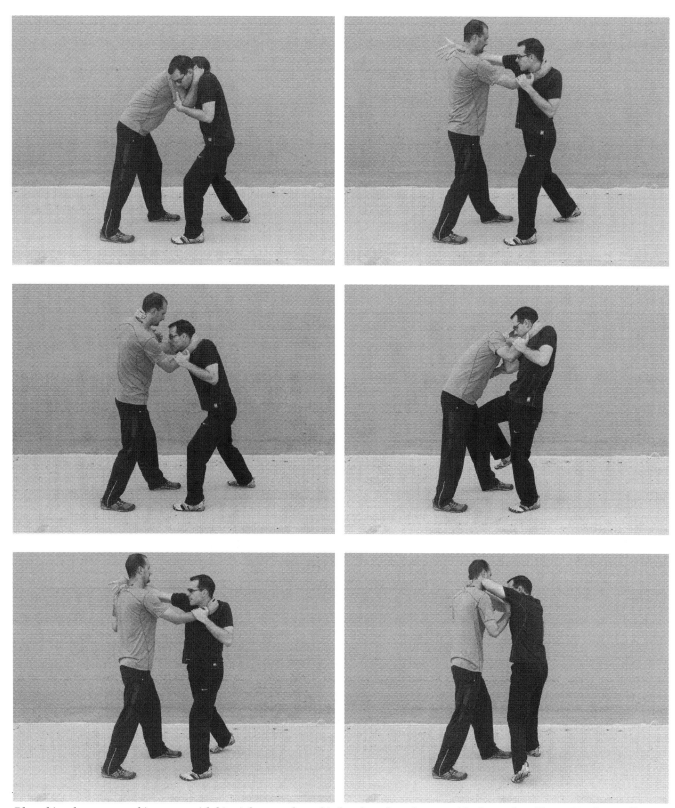

Blue shirt shoves gray shirt away with his right arm, drops his head, and yanks gray shirt into a head butt. He then pulls gray shirt into a knee to the groin before shoving him out again and yanking him into an elbow.

142

The shoving and yanking technique demonstrated in the images to the left is relatively easy to avoid by simply staying close and tight in the clinch. However, many relatively unskilled opponents will be unprepared for the technique, and when it works, in addition to the strikes, the multiple shoves and yanks can be very disorienting. As mentioned previously, the *Control Position* section of the next chapter will cover additional clinch positions and follow ups.

6.6 Ground Fighting

The ground is the last place you want to be in a physical self defense situation. Not only does fighting on the ground generally involve more commitment and more time, but unlike in training rooms, the ground in most places you're likely to be attacked is hard and uneven. Ground fighting on hard surfaces hurts. Additionally, while dealing with multiple opponents is hard no matter what, it's nearly impossible on the ground. In self defense, you should do your absolute best to avoid going to the ground, or putting yourself in a situation where you can be attacked on the ground.

With that said, you do need to learn to fight on the ground. Every serious fight will end with at least one person there. You may get knocked or thrown to the ground, or you may be dragged to the ground by an opponent who is on his way down.

Like fighting in the clinch, ground fighting is all about position. The phrase "position then submission" applies. If you're in an inferior position, you won't be able to effectively use damaging techniques, and your opponent will. So if you do end up on the ground with an opponent, your first priority is to get to a superior position. Also like clinch fighting, if you know what you're doing on the ground, you can make it extremely hard for an attacker or opponent who is relatively unskilled there to strike you, by staying tight and close, even in an inferior position. When your opponent attempts to make the space necessary to strike or slam you, you can use that space to either transition to a superior position, or to apply an attack of your own.

Ground fighting is the area I train least. The amount of positions, transitions, escapes, and submissions is vast, and I feel ground fighting is more difficult to learn from a book than striking or stand-up grappling. Therefore, rather than including instructional photos here, I'm going to recommend that if you haven't already trained in ground fighting, you should seek out a qualified instructor and do so.

Brazilian jiu jitsu (BJJ) is the best system for learning ground *grappling*. But in many pure BJJ schools strikes are not included in the training. Because of that, and because of the emphasis on BJJ competition, many positions and techniques are trained that are *not* practical for self defense. When seeking out an instructor or school, a BJJ school with an MMA emphasis will be better for self defense than a pure BJJ school.

At a minimum, every person interested in physical self defense should know the following in terms of ground fighting:

- How to kick from the ground and stand up safely
- How to escape from the mount, headlock, side mount, knee-in-stomach, and guard
- How to maintain the mount, side mount, knee-in-stomach, and guard
- Attacks and submissions from the mount, side mount, knee-in-stomach, and guard
- How to avoid or counter attacks and submissions from the above positions

The above skills and techniques must be trained with striking included, since in a real self defense situation your opponent probably will be striking you.

6.7 Sparring In The MMA Base

Sparring is the most important training method for the *MMA Base*. There is no *MMA Base* without it. It provides most of the key skills necessary for physical self defense. Through sparring practitioners learn to punch, kick, knee, elbow, and wrestle with an uncooperative opponent, what it is like to hit a person, and what it is like to get hit. But sparring doesn't need to be dangerous. It may seem intimidating or scary for someone who hasn't done it. However with a safe progression beginning with limited techniques and intensity, and moving forward only as practitioners are confident and prepared to do so, it doesn't need to be any more intimidating than any other training drill.

The order of techniques presented in this chapter provides a great way to progress through sparring for a beginner or a martial artist who hasn't sparred much previously. You can begin by sparring only with jabs and catches. After doing so feels comfortable, you can add the cross along with a cover or shoulder roll. The intensity can be kept low, with speed in the low to middle range, but with little follow-through or force on impact. With just a bit of boxing practice at low intensity, you will learn how to gauge and manipulate distance, what is too far and too close, to keep the head down, etc. Adding additional offensive and defensive techniques will become easier and easier, and intensity can be increased safely to a fairly high level of speed and force (with training gear and certain targets off limits).

I recommend using boxing gloves and a mouthpiece for training that is limited to boxing/punching. Once kicking, clinch, and ground are added to the mix, MMA gloves make more sense, and a cup should also be worn to protect the groin.

6.7.1 Sparring Variations

Aside from standard sparring where both practitioners are allowed to use the same techniques, sparring with certain guidelines or limitations can really help to increase skills in a particular area, as well as shed light on certain realities. Here are a few sparring variations you should try:

- Only punching vs. only kicking
- Punching and kicking vs. only kicking
- Grappling only for positional dominance (clinch and/or ground)
- Grappling without striking vs. grappling with striking
- Only stand up striking vs. only stand up grappling/clinch
- Ground fighting submission (starting on the ground) vs. escaping from the ground
- Sparring in natural environments (outdoor or indoors, but not in a training room)
- Offense vs. only defense
- 30 second sparring time limit
- 15 second sparring time limit
- 5 second sparring time limit

After each of the above drills, be sure to discuss what you've learned. Is it harder for someone who is only punching vs. only kicking? Is it harder for someone who is only striking vs. only grappling? How does ground fighting change when one person is only trying to escape? What changes when sparring matches are limited to 5 seconds? What implications do these observations have on self defense?

6.7.2 Sparring Tips

Every practitioner will develop their own fighting style. Some will prefer to stay on the outside with unattached striking, others will prefer grappling. Some will prefer linear footwork, and some angular. Your fighting style will depend largely on your speed, power, body type, and preference. However, there are a number of beneficial, universal concepts that apply to all styles and situations.

Covered Blast

There's already an entire chapter of this book devoted to the *Covered Blast*, but its importance cannot be overstated. Whatever you do and however you fight, stay covered! Use distance to make it impossible for your opponent to reach you. Use position to make it impossible for him to attack you. Use a combination of position and physical cover to keep your vulnerable areas safe. Attack your opponent continuously and in such a way that he is too preoccupied with your attack to be able to attack you. And, combine all of the above.

Control

In the next chapter, I'll go over the details of physical control. It's the key to beating your opponent in both sparring and self defense. If you're not controlling your opponent, then he can control and beat you. You can control your opponent by controlling distance via footwork, position via clinch or ground grappling, and by continuously attacking him.

Example 1: Maintain a safe distance so that your opponent cannot attack you without stepping forward. When he steps forward, you step back with a simple step and slide using the *Cross Footwork* detailed at the beginning of this chapter. Do this a couple of times, baiting your opponent. On his third attempt to get in, rather than stepping back, step in while ducking, and nail him with a low jab or cross, followed by a boxing blast.

Example 2: Use the same strategy as in the first example, but rather than stepping forward and ducking, nail your opponent with a side kick to the knee.

Example 3: Imagine you only have 5 seconds to take out your opponent. Launch a hard, fast, continuous barrage of punches and kicks. If your opponent attempts to counter, don't stop. Move offline or duck while continuing your blast.

Example 4: Change the game frequently. YOU decide when the fight moves from unattached striking to clinching, and back out. If your opponent attempts to change the game, react by changing it again. Make your opponent react to you, and not vice versa.

Constant Offense

One of my boxing instructors once told me to jab at everything. When you move toward your opponent, jab. When your opponent moves toward you, jab. If your opponent jabs, jab. If your opponent attacks with a combination of punches, jab into the combination. Always attack. Continuously attacking, especially into your opponent's attack, will stop him from accomplishing his goals. When you nail your opponent with a jab, follow up with a blast.

Take-Aways

- Train a combination of boxing, kickboxing, Thai boxing and wrestling to develop your skills in attacking and defending against striking and wrestling.
- Start with single techniques drilled in isolation, and progressively add resistance, uncooperativeness, and more techniques to the mix.
- No matter who you are or what you are interested in, if you want to be able to physically defend yourself, you should be comfortable with all areas of the *MMA Base*.

Chapter 7
Functional Self Defense

Functional Self Defense

Training in the *MMA Base* will give you the foundation you need for physical self defense, the delivery systems, understanding, and ability in stand up, clinch, and ground fighting. But as covered in Chapter 5, you need to go beyond the *MMA Base* in order to maximize your self defense skills. MMA training is not only lacking in awareness and prevention, but also in strategy, training, and techniques for self defense. In MMA, both practitioners know when and where the competition will take place. Both parties know the rules. In self defense, there are no rules, and the element of surprise will likely be in play.

The rules that exist in MMA styles, and in the sport of MMA itself, are designed in part to prevent serious injury to the participants. But in physical self defense, the ability to seriously injure your opponent may be exactly what you need.

Chapter 5 covered the aspects of *training* needed for physical self defense that are beyond the *MMA Base*. This chapter covers *techniques* that go beyond the *MMA Base*. These techniques should be integrated into MMA style training, with progressive resistance and against an uncooperative opponent. One great way to train them is to have one practitioner use only techniques from the *MMA Base*, and the other one using the techniques and strategies from this chapter. Keep in mind that more care must be taken with these techniques, as they are typically more dangerous and damaging than those in the *MMA Base*.

Control Positions
This chapter will begin with two control positions that are excellent for self defense, positions that make it easy for you to take out your opponent while avoiding injury to yourself. Along with effective entries to these positions, I will show you various offensive techniques and combinations from these positions.

Entries and the Fundamental Five
In FSD I break the entries into five categories, called the *Fundamental Five*. These five entries also function as default responses and strategies for different types of threats and attacks.

The foundation of the *MMA Base* in combination with more damaging techniques, default responses, and the strategy inherent in the *Fundamental Five*, including the incorporation of the *Covered Blast*, will provide the highest level of skill in physical self defense.

7.1 FSD Control Positions

In the first image, gray shirt has blue shirt in the "Arm Control". In the second image, blue shirt has gray shirt in the "Head And Arm Control".

It's harder to take out an opponent with strikes than you might imagine. Even if you are able to attack someone entirely by surprise, people will quickly and instinctively cover and move away from an attack. I'll relate a story here that I hope will illustrate this concept well, as it did for me when it happened.

For the first four or five years of my training in a karate based style, I learned combination attacks that seemingly made logical sense, but only because I had never actually tried to use them. I was taught that I could strike someone in the face to expose the solar plexus, strike the solar plexus to lower their head and expose their face, and so on, all without moving forward, or without my opponent moving backward.

Once I began sparring, I quickly realized that no one would stand still when under attack. At least, no one but other martial artists who hadn't actually learned how to fight! Around that time, I had also started training in wing chun, and using the wing chun straight blast (a rapid fire, straight line punching blast with forward movement). Against other wing chun practitioners, the straight blast worked very well, because they also responded in ways that made the blast and common follow-ups work. But it wasn't until I got together to spar with a group of martial arts instructors from different styles that I realized that neither prearranged static combinations nor unattached blasting were very effective, and how important physical control was.

In the 1990's, I taught a group class at a local gym, and after my class there was another martial arts class. The instructor asked me if I'd like to meet the next weekend to spar with him and a group of other instructors from around the city. I accepted, and that weekend we met at a boxing ring. I was by far the smallest of the five or six instructors, and I figured I'd need to end the "fight" quickly if I wanted to avoid getting mauled. So in my first round I opened with a wing chun style straight blast. I may have hit my opponent with the first punch, slightly, but his hands immediately covered his face as he quickly moved back and away from me. I continued with the blast, but he stiffly extended his arms, to where I couldn't reach him with any punch. I felt like I had the upper hand in the exchange, but I hadn't really hit him.

I backed off, and he attacked with a combination of kicks, one of which nailed me in the face after I had dropped my hand to block a lower kick first, giving me a bloody lip. However, I was moving away, so it wasn't enough to stop me. I blasted him again, and he covered and moved away again. There were several more exchanges, where neither of us got hit. His blocking in response to my blasting seemed totally unskilled. He reacted as any average person would, moving back and covering. And I felt I had "won". But I never really hit him.

The same thing happened over and over with each instructor. I was able to dominate them with my blasting, and they had no effective way to counter it. They tried to hit me with single attacks or short combinations, and I'd blast them back. But at the end of each round, there was no clear "winner" to all present. Although I felt I had backed them up over and over again, they rightly felt that I hadn't "beaten" them either. When they'd spar each other, there was less blasting and more short striking combinations, where the fighters would often be striking into each others attacks, sometimes both getting hit, but never really effectively. I went home feeling frustrated. Although I had not lost, I surely hadn't won. All of my techniques and training seemed to have no effect at all.

The next time I practiced with my primary training partner, I showed him what had happened, and how my opponent's would cover and move back, in what was actually a very unskilled manner. They'd move back with their arms straightened and fully extended, but between us in such a way that I couldn't hit them. They'd turn away, bend over a bit, and tightly cover their heads. Or, they'd move back and flail around with their arms blocking and in my way. I hadn't seen these unskilled and quite natural reactions before, as I was accustomed to the way other practitioners of my styles would respond. I couldn't hit them. So in the moment, I simply disengaged. But these were very easy positions to attack! However, I had never trained to attack them.

That day, my training partner and I came up with various ways to continue blasting when an opponent would respond in such a way. I switched from using the wing chun "straight blast" to what I simply called "the blast". It was a combination of punches, kicks, knees, and elbows, used in conjunction with physical control. If an opponent would block or cover high, we'd immediately kick low. If his arms were extended so that they were in our way, we'd grab them, yanking the opponent into knee strikes. If he was covering, but tighter, we'd grab the opponent by the back of the neck and arm, and blast him with knees and elbows.

In future sparring matches with other instructors and fighters I met, this new *Blast* worked extremely well. They were accustomed primarily to trading short exchanges of blows and entirely unprepared for a continuous, forward pressure blast that didn't stop with a few punches and kicks, but extended to physical control with knees and elbows. Now, of course, this is common knowledge among any MMA fighter or Thai boxer.

It became obvious to me that in order to quickly and consistently take out an opponent, control was key.

For many years, when teaching new students the *Blast* and explaining the importance of control within it, I'd tell students to try to hit me continuously, and all I'd do is use very unskilled cover or flailing in combination with moving away, to demonstrate how difficult it is to take someone out *without* physically controlling them. If you have any doubt, try it for yourself. Tell a friend or training partner not to let you hit him, only by moving away, extending his arms towards you, and raising his knees to protect against leg kicks.

In physical self defense, keep in mind that if you haven't disabled your opponent, he or she can continue to attack you. Causing your opponent to cover up defensively, but and then attack again, is not success.

Over the years, as I learned and trained more stand up and ground grappling, I realized more and more how important physical control is in self defense. Not only is it difficult to disable an opponent with unattached striking, but without physical control, you cannot apply the most damaging strikes (knees and elbows), and the most damaging techniques of all, joint breaks and chokes.

7.1.1 Head And Arm Control

In the first image, gray shirt has the Head And Arm Control on blue shirt. In the second image, he has transitioned to a more extreme version of the control.

The *Head And Arm Control* is my favorite control position. It's relatively easy to get on an opponent, is very safe, and there are numerous follows-ups or attacks from this position, from throws and locks to strikes and chokes. The first image above shows the standard position. Gray shirt has his left forearm driving forward into blue shirt's neck, and gray shirt's right arm is under blue shirt's left arm, grabbing just above blue shirt's elbow from underneath. Let's take a look at a couple more examples:

In the first image above, you see blue shirt stepping in to get the Head And Arm Control on gray shirt, using the "Smack And Hack" entry (covered later in this chapter). In the second image, you see the control position, where blue shirt has his right arm driving against gray shirt's neck, and his left arm wrapping under gray shirt's right arm. Notice how blue shirt's left hand grabs just above gray shirt's elbow. Notice also that blue shirt has his left foot forward. The forward leg in the finished control position is the leg opposite the arm that drives against the neck.

The key to applying the *Head And Arm Control* is pressure. The arm that controls the opponent's head, or the hacking arm, should always be driving into the opponent's neck with the bone at the outer edge of your forearm. This pressure is initially aided with a forward step, as demonstrated in the images at left. Blue shirt steps forward ***twice***. With the first step he sets up the position, creating a path for it by moving gray shirt's arm out of the way for the hacking arm. With the second step he drives gray shirt backward, pressuring with the hacking arm, and wrapping or snaking his left hand and arm underneath gray shirt's right arm. The "arm control" arm should be pulling or sucking the opponent's arm toward you, with pulling pressure on the opponent's arm just above his elbow. The *Head And Arm Control* involves simultaneously pushing and pulling pressure.

Blue shirt demonstrates how even in the first step of the Head And Arm Control, he is safe against gray shirt's punching attempts. Of course in reality, he would have immediately taken the second step with his right foot to drive gray shirt back further.

The *Head And Arm Control* may appear at first glance to be difficult to apply against a much larger opponent, but it is surprisingly easy with the proper pressure and structure. Rather than using the muscles of your arm to pressure your opponent's head and neck, you must focus on using the alignment of your bones. When taking the second step to drive your opponent back and applying the simultaneous pushing (on the neck) and pulling (on the arm) pressure, *do not bend your arm and attempt to push your opponent with the muscles of your hacking arm.* Maintain the same relaxed and slightly bent elbow position throughout the step. Use your legs to drive forward, and use the structure of the bones of your hacking arm to drive your opponent back, as if there was an unbendable metal rod attached to your shoulder.

Notice that in all of the images on the previous page, that the elbow of the hacking arm is slightly bent. If it is bent too far, it will engage and require primarily muscular tension to keep extended, and this will not work against a stronger opponent. But if the arm is completely straightened, you will not be able to exert pressure on the opponent's neck, and the opponent will easily be able to pop your arm up with his free hand, duck under, and grab you in a bear hug or clinch.

Although the arm that wraps around your opponent's arm should be firm and exerting a pulling pressure, it must also be relaxed enough to move with your opponent's attempts to escape. If your arm is too loose, your opponent can easily pull his arm out. If it is too tense, he will also be able to get it out, by moving around your tension. The key is to pull his arm and elbow toward you almost as if you are hanging on his arm in a sticky way. Stick to his arm, and follow it where it goes.

Head And Arm Control: Striking Follow Ups

From the Head And Arm Control, knee strikes to the groin or solar plexus are easy, but difficult for your opponent to effectively block. If your opponent is bent over and nearly taken out by your knee strikes, you can release the hold to launch a powerful elbow to his temple or jaw.

There are many possible and very effective follow ups or attacks from the *Head And Arm Control*. I tend to begin each control with a knee to the groin or solar plexus, to loosen my opponent up and/or keep him on defense. In the images above, blue shirt grabs the back of gray shirt's neck to pull him into the knee to the groin. Keep in mind that gray shirt could attempt to grab the knee and/or drop under blue shirt's arm to tackle or take him down. Blue shirt must be ready to quickly bring his kneeing leg back and drop his lead elbow down to prevent gray shirt from succeeding. When dropping the elbow to prevent a successful takedown or clinch attempt, the key is to also drive the bone of the hacking arm into gray shirt's neck, to stretch him out and re-create the *Head And Arm Control* position.

Head And Arm Control: The Duck Under

Gray shirt attempts to put blue shirt in a head lock immediately as blue shirt applies the Head And Arm Control. This is a common response. Blue shirt simply ducks under gray shirt's arm, maintaining the position of his hand on gray shirt's neck. Blue shirt throws his right arm over gray shirt's shoulder, grabbing his right wrist with his left hand, securing the "harness". He can then easily throw gray shirt to the ground, or bring him down gently and into a choke. The duck under follow-up can be used even if gray shirt does not attempt to use the head lock.

The duck under is an excellent follow-up to the *Head And Arm Control*. Although it works perfectly when an opponent attempts to put you in a head lock, it can also be a great technique to use without the head lock attempt. As demonstrated in the images on the previous page, the duck under can easily lead to the *harness*, from which you can throw or choke your opponent easily.

As demonstrated in the following images, the duck under will also put you in a position that allows you to grab your opponent's face and sling or slam him to the ground. **Face grabs and head wrenches/ manipulations can be extremely dangerous, even lethal. Take extreme care when practicing them. Never twist or wrench your opponent's head quickly, or beyond the point of slight muscular tension.**

Blue shirt demonstrates two types of face grabs following the duck under.

Head And Arm Control: Kimura

Blue shirt uses the kimura or "bent arm lock" against gray shirt from the Head And Arm Control.

The *kimura*, or bent arm lock, works very well from the *Head And Arm Control*. In the images above, blue shirt uses his left (hacking) arm to grab just above gray shirt's elbow, and to assist his right hand and arm in applying the *kimura*. Notice that he shifts his body to generate more pulling power. The kimura can be used to throw gray shirt into a wall or object, or if applied quickly and forcefully, to break his shoulder. In the following images, blue shirt uses the *kimura* to bring gray shirt to the ground:

Head And Arm Control: Slings And Throws

Blue shirt enters into the Head And Arm Control and quickly steps twice to spin 180 degrees, taking gray shirt with him and slamming gray shirt's head into a wall. He then knees gray shirt in the face or ribs, and can break gray shirt's shoulder with the "kimura".

A variety of slings and throws can be applied from the *Head And Arm Control*, many of which can disable your opponent by slamming him into the ground or into a wall, car, or other solid object. Although most of the throws demonstrated here can be used no matter how your opponent is resisting, going with his energy or resistance will require less force and will be easier to apply.

Throws can also work particularly well when your opponent attempts to prevent you from applying other techniques. For example, if you've gotten your opponent in the *Head And Arm Control* and his arm is too low and tight to allow for the duck under, the following throw works very well:

Gray shirt's left arm is too low and tense for blue shirt to duck under it, so blue shirt turns gray shirt's head as he steps behind and throws him to the ground. In the images above, blue shirt only brings gray shirt down to his butt. **In an extreme situation, blue shirt could slam gray shirt's head into the ground, with all of his weight driving gray shirt's head into the concrete. However, this could easily kill gray shirt, and should not be attempted except in life or death self defense situations.**

Although gray shirt should not be able to grab blue shirt's lead leg, due to the position of blue shirt's forearm and elbow this throw can work well if he attempts to. As gray shirt goes for blue shirt's lead leg, blue shirt steps back, drives gray shirt's head down, and simultaneously pulls his arm around clockwise. Gray shirt ends up on the ground where blue shirt can escape or strike gray shirt.

In the images above, blue shirt shifts and yanks gray shirt into a simple throw to the ground. He can either continue the circular momentum of the second image, or shove gray shirt forward and to the ground.

Head And Arm Control: Holds

In the second image above, gray shirt applies the "kimura" on blue shirt. He then grabs blue shirt's face with his left hand, bringing blue shirt up into a combination head wrench and arm lock.

The *Head And Arm Control* is not designed to be a static control position. Although pressure is applied to the neck, head, and arm, the purpose of the control is to facilitate striking, locking, choking, and throwing. The *Head And Arm Control* is designed to provide you with cover, as you disable your opponent, not as a "hold". There are a few holds that can be applied from the *Head And Arm Control*, however. The hold on the previous page can work well, as can bringing your opponent to the ground with a kimura, or using a modified version of the *Head And Arm Control*:

7.1.2 Arm Control

In the first image, gray shirt has blue shirt in the Arm Control. In the second image, blue shirt has gray shirt in the Arm Control and is pulling him into a knee to the solar plexus.

The *Arm Control* may look simple and relatively ineffective. However, it is an extremely effective control that leads to a great variety of follow-ups and attacks. The *Arm Control* involves having one hand grabbing the opponent's wrist, and the other grabbing just above his elbow. Notice the position of gray shirt's hands in the first image above. The hand grabbing blue shirt's wrist is palm-down or in, and the hand grabbing just above blue shirt's elbow is palm-up or out. Many beginners and practitioners of other martial arts have a tendency to grab with both hands in the same position (palms down/out), but this leads to a much weaker control that can be easily escaped from. Imagine grabbing a thick rope with two hands, with something very heavy on the other end that must be pulled. You would always position your hands with your palms facing opposite directions. The *Arm Control* should be no different.

From the Arm Control it is surprisingly easy to pull and shove a much larger opponent backwards and forwards, and surprisingly difficult for him to escape (as long as your hands are in the right position!). Pulling your opponent forward makes it impossible for him to strike you with his rear hand due to the alignment of his body relative to yours. Even if your opponent has his arm bent, the control works. And even if he is so large and strong that you cannot move him, by pulling, you'll end up moving yourself to a safe position relative to his body. On the following pages, you'll find a number of possible follow ups from the *Arm Control*.

Arm Control: Knees And Elbows

Blue shirt yanks gray shirt into a knee to the groin. As he brings his knee down, he pivots and drops his weight into an elbow strike to gray shirt's arm, just above gray shirt's elbow. This can easily break gray shirt's elbow. If gray shirt was shorter, blue shirt may have elbowed him in the head instead. After the first elbow, blue shirt clears gray shirt's arm and elbows him in the face. He then yanks him into a knee to the solar plexus, followed by another elbow to the head.

Blue shirt yanks gray shirt into an elbow to the face.

The previous two series of pictures are examples of ways to use knees and elbows from the *Arm Control*. They are not meant as prearranged combinations. From the *Arm Control*, you can pull your opponent into knees or elbows, and follow with many different combinations of knees and elbows, depending on your opponent's position. Try a variety of different combinations with your training partners, and pay attention to which ones work best in different situations and with different sized partners.

Arm Control: Face Grabs And Head Manipulations

From the *Arm Control*, it's easy to grab your opponent's face after quickly pulling his arm toward you. As mentioned in the previous section on the *Head And Arm Control*, **twisting an opponent's head can be extremely dangerous and lethal. It should only be done in extreme situations, and great care must be taken when practicing such techniques with a partner.** Never turn or twist your partner's head quickly, and never beyond the point where you feel even slight tension.

Blue shirt yanks gray shirt into him and quickly switches to a face grab. His right hand grabs gray shirt's face, and his left hand grabs the back of gray shirt's head. From this position blue shirt can easily slam gray shirt to the ground, transition to a choke, or do extreme damage to gray shirt's neck.

Gray shirt pulls blue shirt forward, switching his "near hand" to the back of blue shirt's head, maintaining the pulling motion and pressure. He then uses his "far hand" to turn blue shirt's head, and elbows him in the face. From this position he can easily throw blue shirt to the ground by his head.

Kness, elbows, face grabs, throws, and chokes are the easiest and most reliable follow-ups to the *Arm Control*. For those who have practiced martial arts that focus on joint manipulations (ju jutsu, aikido, etc.), there are many other possible follow-ups that can be used. In addition, against a similar sized opponent, the Arm Control itself can be used to yank and shove your opponent into objects, or to simply throw him or her away from you.

7.2 FSD Fundamental Five

The FSD *Fundamental Five* is a combination of physical self defense strategy, extremely effective default response techniques, and the *Covered Blast* concept, designed to be applied in five different threat or attack situations.

1. Hit And Run: The *Hit And Run* is ideal when you can quickly escape, but must distract your attacker before doing so. If you're alone with your attacker but very near to a safe place, or if you only need a bit of space in order to escape, the *Hit And Run* is a great option. It can also be used as a "feeler", as an attack with a low level of commitment and high level of safety.

2. Blast: The *Blast* is ideal when you must completely disable your opponent before escaping. If you're with family members who cannot run or escape, if you're in an isolated area and far from safety, and the only way you can survive is to take your attacker out, the *Blast* is the way to go.

3. Crash: The *Hit And Run* and the *Blast* are primarily offensive, whereas the *Crash* is a defensive response, or more accurately, a "counter-offensive" response. The *Crash* is a default response designed to be used against a striking attack, and can be followed with a *Hit And Run* or *Blast* strategy.

4. Takedown Defense: The *Takedown Defense* is another defensive response, designed to be used when an attacker attempts to tackle you or enter into grappling. It is also followed with either a *Hit And Run* or *Blast* strategy.

5. Clinch Entry: The *Clinch Entry* is a counter-offensive strategy to be used when you're in trouble, when you're getting pounded and don't have the footing to resort to the *Crash*. It involves quickly changing the game and getting back to a position of control.

In the rest of this section, I'll cover technical default responses for each of the *Fundamental Five*. These are the responses that my students and I have found to be the most efficient and effective, but they are not the only options! The most important part of the *Fundamental Five* is the existence and use of the physical strategy combined with the *Covered Blast* concept.

Combining a physical self defense strategy with default responses that work well against a wide variety of attacks will dramatically increase your odds of success in a physical confrontation. That's what the *Fundamental Five* are about.

7.2.1 Hit And Run

Blue shirt nails gray shirt in the groin and runs.

The *Hit And Run* is ideal when you are threatened, but feel that you can quickly escape with the aid of a technique that temporarily occupies or disables your opponent. For example, if you've turned a corner off of a crowded street onto a side street with few people and an attacker blocks your path and tells you to come with him, then a *Hit And Run* to safety may be the prefect option.

I first named this strategy "Injure The Corners", based on a strategy from the *Book of Five Rings* by Miyamoto Musashi, the famous Japanese swordsman. Musashi writes:

> *"It is difficult to move strong things by pushing directly, so you should "injure the corners". In single combat, it is easy to win once the enemy collapses. This happens when you injure the "corners" of his body, and thus weaken him. It is important to know how to do this, so you must research deeply."*

The *Hit And Run* can also be thought of as a way to "injure the corners". It can be used to facilitate a quick escape, or to injure your opponent without attacking him head-on, avoiding a significant commitment. In either case, the key to making the *Hit And Run* work is to attack your opponent in such a way that his options for a counter attack are minimized. **You want to be able to nail your opponent while moving away from him.** This is difficult to effectively do with most techniques from the *MMA Base*. But it can be achieved with more damaging techniques to extremely vulnerable targets such as the eyes and groin. These targets do not require a high level of force to be damaged, and can be attacked while "passing by".

Triangular footwork is ideal for the *Hit And Run*, as it brings you to the outside of your opponent's reach while still giving you forward momentum and force for your attack.

Hit And Run: Eye Strike

Blue shirt attacks gray shirt with an eye strike. Notice how blue shirt uses triangular footwork to move away from gray shirt as he strikes.

There is no better technique for the *Hit And Run* than the eye strike, assuming it is properly executed. The eye is extraordinarily fragile and easy to damage, no matter how large or strong your opponent is. I've hit two people in the eye, and they were both instantly disabled. I've also been accidentally hit in the eye myself, by a student. Not only was it extremely painful, but I was unable to open either of my eyes fully, and had to be driven to a hospital. My student's fingernail had gouged my cornea, and I had to have drops put into my eyes every half hour for 48 hours and wear a patch for a long time. A proper eye strike is an amazingly effective self defense technique.

Note: The eye strike is also incredibly dangerous. **It should not be used unless your opponent poses a real and substantial physical threat to you or someone you care about, and there must be no other way to escape.** It is possible to permanently blind your opponent by striking him in the eye, and would not be morally or legally acceptable against anything but the most serious threat.

The key to executing a prefect, effective, covered eye strike is to use a backhanded sweeping motion. Notice in the images above how blue shirt steps out to his left and uses a right backhanded sweeping eye strike. His head is largely covered by his right arm and shoulder. The sweeping motion of the eye strike is easier to land, because it travels along a horizontal plane. A straight line motion like a finger jab to the eye is much more difficult to land, because it requires you to accurately strike a small target both horizontally and vertically.

The aim is to use the nail of your middle finger to slice and gouge into your opponent's eye. Even if you have very short finger nails and only your finger tip strikes the eye, it can be both damaging and disabling for your opponent.

The eye strike should only be trained against a partner wearing safety goggles. ***Do not train the eye strike with a partner who is not wearing safety goggles!*** I have made the mistake, and trust me, it is not worth it. It only takes a slight mistake or shift to accidentally get injured or injure your partner. You can purchase safety goggles for a couple of dollars at any home improvement or hardware store.

Train the eye strike as you would any other technique. Use it in the context of sparring, in different scenarios, and try it against an opponent who is fighting you with the techniques of the *MMA Base*.

Blue shirt demonstrates the eye strike from another angle. Notice how he uses triangular footwork, stepping out and away with his right foot while executing a right backhanded sweeping attack. His head is covered by his right arm and shoulder.

The incorrect way to do an eye strike. Here, blue shirt simply jabs his fingers forward to gray shirt's eye. Notice how easy it is for gray shirt to simultaneously strike blue shirt in the face.

With proper form, the eye strike can be used against a punching attack. It can both cover the practitioner against a punch, and knock a punch offline, functioning as a block.

Hit And Run: Groin Slap

Blue shirt attacks gray shirt with a groin slap, and runs away.

The groin slap is very similar to the eye strike in terms of execution. Both use the same outward triangular step, giving the practitioner the opportunity to run away immediately after the strike. However, in my experience the groin slap is less reliable than the eye strike. When I've hit people in the groin, it has always instantly disabled them. But I've been struck in the groin numerous times and continued fighting. On the other hand, it nearly always causes a reaction of some sort. Typically the receiver will at least drop his hands and bend over a bit.

Although I've only bowled once or twice in my life, I compare the motion of the groin slap to bowling. Imagine you are trying to bowl through your opponent's groin. The aim is to fully slap and crush his testicles with a heavy, powerful, open handed slap. After the initial impact, you can also grab, crush, and yank. If your opponent's hands are raised when you execute the groin slap, you should use your free hand to parry or slap his lead hand to the side. This will make it more difficult for him to block the groin slap, and prevents him from punching you in the face on your way in (see the following images).

The groin slap should be practiced on a training partner wearing a protective cup. Train it in the context of a *Hit And Run* scenario, and against an opponent who is using the techniques of the *MMA Base*.

Blue shirt steps into gray shirt and slaps his lead arm up and out of the way as he nails gray shirt with a groin slap. He follows up with a downward slap to the ear, from which he can easily run.

The images above demonstrate the groin slap from another angle. Notice how blue shirt "scoops" gray shirt's left arm up and by, right above gray shirt's elbow, as he moves in for the groin slap. This helps to ensure that gray shirt cannot block the groin slap or strike blue shirt. In these images, the parry/trap/scoop is shown as a separate step, but in reality it comes right before the groin slap itself.

Hit And Run: The Side Kick

Blue shirt attacks gray shirt with a side kick, using the "Hit And Run" strategy.

Although I prefer the eye strike and the groin slap for the *Hit And Run*, a quick and hard side kick can also work very well, particularly against a similar or smaller sized opponent. The problem with the side kick against a larger opponent, particularly if he has greater reach, is that he may be able to punch through the side kick and still hit you. The side kick doesn't offer nearly as much positional protection as the eye strike or groin slap, and in my experience. It is less likely to be as effective.

To make the side kick work, the ideal target is just above the front of the attacker's knee, driving the outer edge of your foot through his leg at a slight downward angle. Kicking the side of the knee makes it easy for the attacker to bend his knee away from the kick and avoid damage. Kicking at a downward angle helps to jam his foot into the ground, making it harder for him to move his foot back or away to avoid the force of the kick. The attacker's knee must also be relatively straight. If it is bent too deeply, you will not have the angle necessary to hyper-extend the joint.

7.2.2 The Blast

The *Blast* is what you use when you must completely disable your opponent. Like the *Hit And Run*, it is not a specific technique, but a strategy. The *Blast* involves a continuous, unrelenting attack. It doesn't stop until your opponent is disabled.

As with the *Hit And Run* and all strategies of the *Fundamental Five*, using the concept of the *Covered Blast* (see Chapter 4) is extremely important. Throughout your *Blast*, you should be maximally covered to avoid getting nailed by your opponent as you attempt to take him out. The *Blast* is not simply a crazy, uncoordinated barrage of strikes. It is a well designed and covered, continuous attack.

Although the *Blast* is an attack, ideally used before your opponent's attack, it can also be used as an interception, a counter-offensive response to your opponent's attack. The *Blast* can begin with literally any technique, but some techniques are more effective than others in terms of providing cover, the ability to continue the attack, and the ability to quickly gain control of your opponent. In this section I'll demonstrate the entry techniques and combinations I've found to be the most efficient and effective, leading to the control positions shown at the beginning of this chapter. ***Please refer back to the section on control positions for follow ups to the entry techniques demonstrated here.***

The Blast: Smack And Hack Entry

Blue shirt uses the Smack And Hack to attack gray shirt and ends with gray shirt in the Head And Arm Control position. Notice how blue shirt steps forward with his right foot as he nails gray shirt with the Smack And Hack, and then steps forward again with his left foot as he drives gray shirt back into the Head And Arm Control.

If I had to choose a favorite self defense technique, it would likely be what I call the *Smack And Hack*. The *Smack And Hack* alone is likely to take an opponent out, but if it doesn't, it gives you my favorite control position, the *Head And Arm Control*, from which *Blasting* your opponent with the most effective follow ups is easy. The *Smack And Hack* is the ideal covered entry for the *Blast*.

Note: **The *Smack And Hack* is a dangerous technique that should only be used in a serious self defense situation. Striking the neck can be lethal. Do not use this technique in sparring or against a training partner.**

The *Smack And Hack* consists of a forward step and drive into your opponent, ideally using a forward triangular step from a slight outside position, while "smacking" your opponent's lead arm out of your way and "hacking" him in the front side of his neck with the bone on the outside of your forearm.

The "smack" serves three purposes. First, it stops your opponent from being able to hit you with his lead hand on your way in. Second, it prevents him from using his lead hand or arm to block your attack. And third, it can function as a surprising shock that mentally disrupts your opponent. The smack should be fast, hard, and painful.

Gray shirt attacks blue shirt with the Smack And Hack. Notice how gray shirt wraps his right arm under blue shirt's left arm, grabbing his arm just above the elbow, as he drives blue shirt backward into the Head And Arm Control after the hack. He follows up with a knee to blue shirt's solar plexus.

The "hack" is a fast, powerful, and extremely effective technique, particularly when used against the front side of your opponent's neck. The hack is not meant to be used against your opponent's throat, or against the side of his neck. The target is the front "quarter", or the front-side of the neck, the brachial plexus. The hack uses the outer edge of your forearm bone to slam into your opponent's neck with both an outward and forward motion. Your entire body should be used to drive the hack, pushing through with the rear foot. Practice it against a heavy bag or focus mitts, and you'll see how powerful the hack can be. It can easily knock out a much larger and stronger opponent.

The *Smack And Hack* entry ends with the *Head And Arm Control*. It requires two steps to be taken, and the steps should be done in one fluid motion. The first step brings you into your opponent as you attack with the *Smack And Hack* itself. The second step drives your opponent backward as you secure the *Head And Arm Control*. Many beginners make the mistake of collapsing the hacking arm as they take the second step. Instead, the solid structure of the hacking arm must be maintained. You should drive your opponent backward with the structural alignment of the bones in your arm, rather than with muscular strength, and your step forward should directly translate into the same amount of drive into your opponent's neck.

Blue shirt demonstrates how the Smack And Hack keeps him covered against gray shirt's striking attempt.

Just as the smack protects you against your opponent's lead hand, the hack should protect you from your opponent's rear hand. Notice in the images above how gray shirt's punching attack is blocked by blue shirt's arm. Although blue shirt has dropped his head further in response to gray shirt's punching attack, the position of his hacking arm and the pressure of his arm against gray shirt's neck will prevent any solid punch from landing.

Gray shirt attacks blue shirt with the Smack And Hack. Pay attention to gray shirt's footwork. His first step is forward and into blue shirt. His second step is forward and slightly outward.

Your opponent may attempt to block the hack with his rear hand, however it is unlikely that the block will completely stop the hack, due to the power of the hack and the angle of the attack. The beauty of the technique is that even if your opponent is able to block the hack with his read hand, you will still be able to move directly into the *Head And Arm Control*. There are many possible follow-ups to the *Smack And Hack* entry that allow you to maintain the superior *Head And Arm Control* position, demonstrated earlier in this chapter. My general preference is to throw one knee either to the groin or the solar plexus, just after getting the *Head And Arm Control*. If your *Smack And Hack* fails and you are unable to move to the *Head And Arm Control*, you should be able to seamlessly flow into the *Blast* entry in the following section.

The Blast: Palm Blast Entry

The *Palm Blast* entry is a modified version of the boxing blast, demonstrated in the *MMA Base* chapter, but better suited to self defense. Rather than using punches, palm strikes are used. As with the *Smack And Hack*, the goal of the *Palm Blast* is either to take your opponent out, or to end up in a control position from which you can more easily do so. To maximize the pressure you put on your opponent, the *Palm Blast* should use the "alternating crosses" footwork beginning after the first rear handed palm strike. However, alternative strikes that are not used in boxing can be added, still using the alternating crosses footwork, for example, the groin slap:

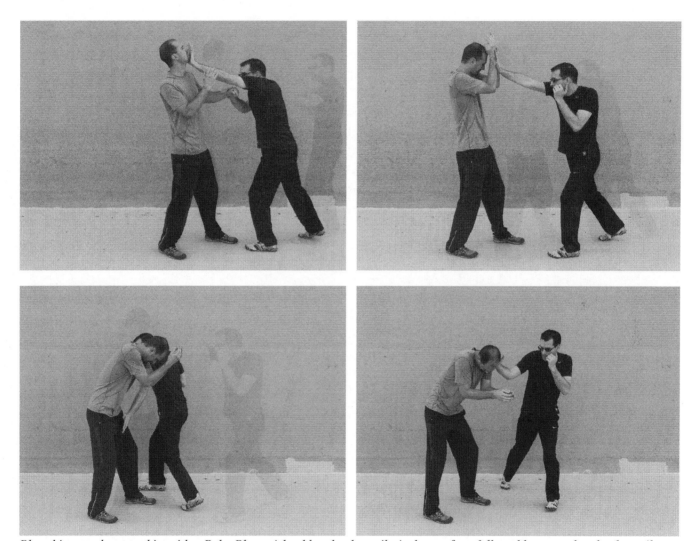

Blue shirt attacks gray shirt with a Palm Blast. A lead hand palm strike is thrown first, followed by a rear hand palm strike, using a jab - cross structure from boxing. After the cross, blue shirt uses the "alternating crosses" footwork, stepping forward deeply and using another rear handed strike, this time a groin slap. This can be followed with strikes or a control position.

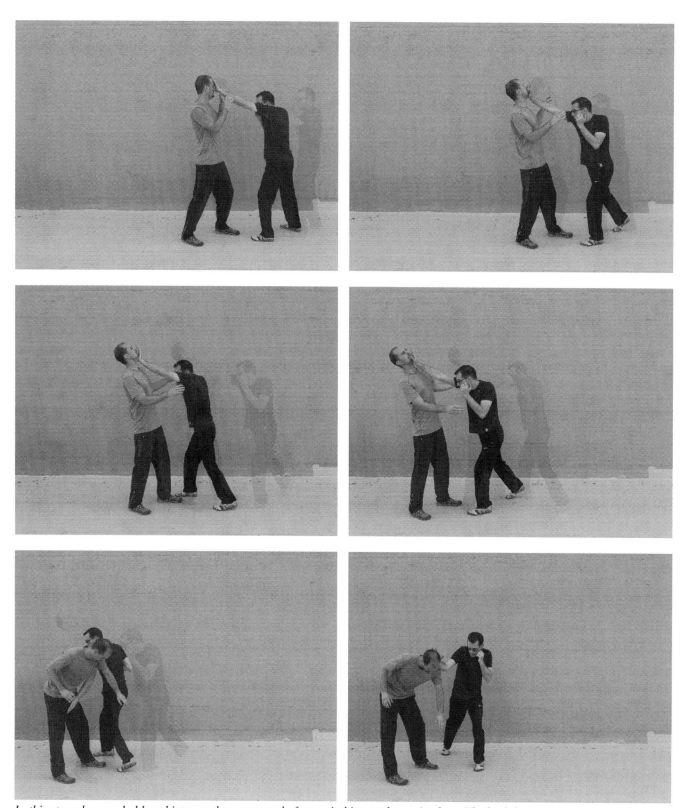

In this staged example blue shirt uses three crosses before switching to the groin slap. The high line palm strikes are often a good set up for the low line groin slap. Obviously, no one will stand still and allow you to continuously strike them in the face. The above example is purely an illustration of the "alternating crosses" footwork leading to the groin slap.

The *Palm Blast* entry can also be used as an interception if your opponent has attacked first, or if he has attempted to counter-punch during your blast. For low line attacks to softer targets, punches should be used instead of palms. In the following example, blue shirt uses a low jab as the first strike in his blast, to intercept gray shirt's attack. This intercepting version can also be used if your opponent attempts to counter punch during a *Palm Blast* that you have initiated first.

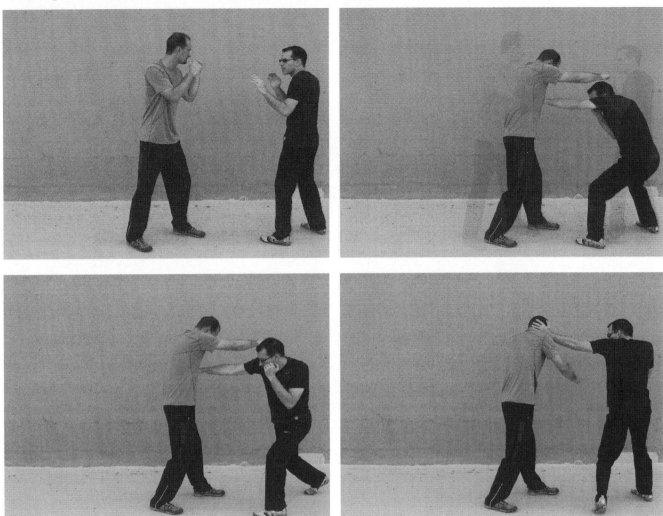

Continued on next page…

Gray shirt attempts to attack blue shirt, but blue shirt intercepts with a Palm Blast. Blue shirt ducks to avoid the attack while simultaneously using a low jab - low cross combination. He then uses a high open hand hook, a high palm cross, and a forward step with a groin kick, then an open handed strike/slap to gray shirt's ear, and a knee to the face.

As demonstrated in the previous series, kicks can also be used with the *Palm Blast* entry. The following example shows a low cross intercept and includes kicks, knees, and elbows:

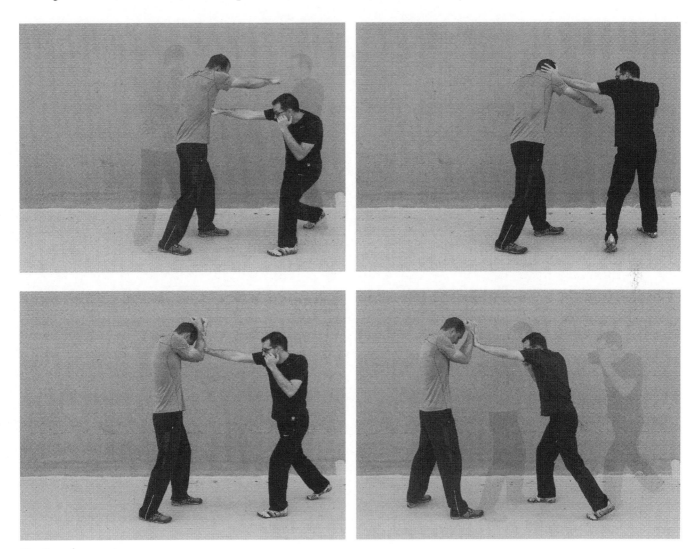

Continued on next page...

Starting on the previous page, gray shirt attacks blue shirt with a high cross. Blue shirt drops and intercepts with a low cross. The cross is followed by a high open hand hook and two alternating palm crosses. Because gray shirt covers in response to the Palm Blast entry, blue shirt continues his Blast with a Thai kick to the thigh, followed by an elbow - knee - elbow combination.

Thus far, the *Palm Blast* entry has only been demonstrated with striking follow-ups. However, both the *Head And Arm Control* and the *Arm Control* can be used after the *Palm Blast* entry. Many opponents will naturally cover their head or turn away from a high striking attack. This provides the opportunity to grab your opponent with the *Head And Arm Control*. Other opponents may extend their arms straight out at face level to avoid your strikes. This provides the opportunity to grab an outstretched arm, getting the *Arm Control*.

In the vast majority of cases, after beginning your *Palm Blast* (including the low punching intercept) you will either be able to groin slap, groin kick, Thai kick, or grab your opponent with the *Head And Arm Control* or the *Arm Control*. All of these follow-ups can then be followed with more powerful knees and elbows, or joint breaks and chokes. The key is to train them all. Practice attacking your partner with the Palm Blast, and flowing into striking or controlling follow-ups, with additional "finishing" techniques. You should notice that certain positions and reactions create different opportunities. If your opponent is moving backward quickly but flailing his arms, kicks may work better than controls. If your opponent hunkers down and covers, moving to a control position may work better. The leg your opponent has forward and your weight distribution will also determine which kick you have available (Thai kick or groin kick).

In the following examples, blue shirt gets to the control positions from the *Palm Blast*:

Blue shirt attacks gray shirt with a Palm Blast, but quickly steps in and grabs gray shirt with the "Head And Arm Control", followed by a knee strike. Notice that blue shirt's head is covered by his arm in the "Head And Arm Control" entry.

Blue shirt attacks gray shirt with a Palm Blast. When gray shirt raises his arms to cover against the Blast, blue shirt grabs an arm and puts gray shirt in the Arm Control. He follows up with a combination of knees and elbows.

The *Palm Blast* and follow-ups can and should be trained in the context of sparring. In the following images, a boxing variation is demonstrated:

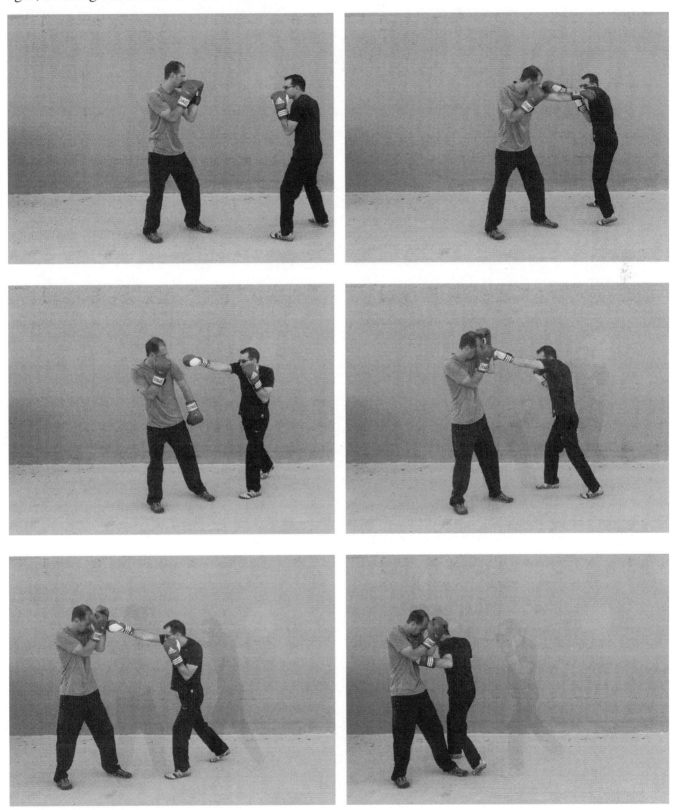

Continued on next page...

Beginning on the previous page, blue shirt side steps and counter jabs against gray shirt's jab. He then follows up with 3 alternating crosses. Instead of using the groin slap, blue shirt uses an upper cut - hook combination, stepping deeply through gray shirt, and follows with a final cross.

The *Smack And Hack* and *Palm Blast* are both excellent *Blast* entries. Both can take out your opponent on their own, or via the control positions that easily follow. My default attack is the *Smack And Hack*. I save the *Palm Blast* for interceptions and when things go wrong. You can use either, or if you have another efficient and effective *Blast* entry you prefer, you can use that instead. The key is to have something. You need a default response to a physical threat you're unable to escape from. You may have to vary the response based on distance, position, the number of opponents, or environmental conditions. But having a single response that will work in a high percentage of situations and against a high percentage of opponents will ensure you don't get stuck in a mental "analysis paralysis". If you can't escape and you must act, it's best to have a plan in the form of a simple and functional default response.

The *Smack And Hack* and the *Palm Blast* entries both follow the *Covered Blast* concept. The *Smack And Hack* uses a combination of trapping, attacking, physical cover, and relative position to keep you as safe as possible while nailing your opponent. The follow-ups, from the *Head And Arm Control*, use a combination of physical control, cover, relative position, and attacking. The *Palm Blast*, using boxing form, utilizes a combination of physical cover and attacking to keep your opponent on defense while you remain on offense. And the follow-ups from the *Head And Arm Control* or the *Arm Control* use physical control, cover, relative position, and attacking. If you do choose to use a different *Blast* entry as your default response, make sure it also follows the *Covered Blast* concept.

7.2.3 The Crash

Blue shirt attacks gray shirt with a right cross. Gray shirt counters with the Crash, jamming blue shirts attack and yanking him into an Arm Control followed by a knee strike.

The *Crash* is an incredibly effective default response that works against the vast majority of punching attacks. It doesn't matter whether your opponent attacks with a straight right, a straight left, a right hook, or a left hook. It doesn't matter if he's only attacking with a single punch, or a combination of punches. And, you don't need to determine which punch is coming in. When your opponent begins his attack, you simply crash in, jam his attack, potentially injure his face with the *Crash* itself, and immediately establish either the *Head And Arm Control* or the *Arm Control*. The harder your opponent attacks, the better the *Crash* works.

The *Crash* is simple. Drop your head a bit, raise both of your forearms to cover your head, one on top of the other (not crossing your arms), and ram your opponent in the face. It should be one single action. Your head drops as your arms come up as you drive forward into your opponent. No matter how your opponent attacks or which punch or punches he throws, attempt to ram his face. Do not target his arms. Target his face.

When you *Crash*, you'll either end up ramming into your opponent's arms or his face, depending on how he attacks. If you ram his arms, grab one of them and yank him into the *Arm Control*. If you ram his face, grab him behind the neck and pull him into the *Head And Arm Control* as you knee him in the groin or solar plexus. Here is an example of the *Crash* used against a right hook:

Gray shirt attacks blue shirt with a right hook. Blue shirt Crashes, ramming gray shirt in the face, and gets the Head And Arm Control from which he can use any of the follow-ups demonstrated earlier in this chapter.

In the images above, blue shirt's left arm wraps under gray shirt's right arm to secure the *Head And Arm Control*. It's also possible to use an "over-wrap", for a variation of the *Head And Arm Control*:

Gray shirt uses the Crash against blue shirt's right hook, and wraps his right arm over instead of under. While the over-wrap still allows a variety of follow-ups, we prefer the under-wrap.

My preference is to wrap under my opponent's arm for the *Head And Arm Control*, rather than wrapping over his arm. From the over-wrap, knees, elbows, and throws are possible. However, there are more options from the under-wrap position, including the duck-under, and your opponent will have a harder time fighting back. To ensure you can get the under-wrap, simply move the arm that will go against your opponent's neck slightly before the arm that will wrap:

Gray shirt uses the Crash against blue shirt's right hook. In order to secure the under-wrap instead of the over-wrap, gray shirt drives his right arm into blue shirt's neck JUST before wrapping his arm under blue shirt's arm. This slight delay makes it easier and more natural to thread his left arm underneath blue shirt's arm.

Notice in all of the *Crash* sequences above that the practitioner using the *Crash* steps forward and into the attacker. **The *Crash* will not work if this aggressive forward step is not taken**, as your opponent will not have his attack jammed, he will not be off balance, and he will easily be able to move around you and hit you with follow-up strikes. The two most important components of the *Crash* are the solid cover and the forward drive/step with jamming pressure. The forward pressure it what causes your arms to "stick" to your opponent for an instant, just long enough to yank him into either the *Head And Arm Control* or the *Arm Control*.

The *Crash* is an interception. Therefore it should not be used before your opponent moves to attack, or at the end of his attack, but into his attack. To do this, maintain a safe distance from your opponent, so that he cannot reach you without stepping forward. As soon as he begins his step forward to attack you, drive forward and ram him in the face like a freight train. Stepping forward simultaneously will cut the "contact time" in half and at least double the force of the opponent's attack, directly into his face.

If your opponent throws a hook, or if you end up under his arm after crashing a straight punch, your arm that wraps his arm should be on the same side as his punching arm.

- If your opponent throws a right hook and you *Crash* into his face, use your right arm to apply pressure against his neck and your left arm to under-wrap his hooking arm.

- If your opponent throws a left hook and you *Crash* into his face, use your left arm to apply pressure against his neck and your right arm to under-wrap his hooking arm.

If your opponent throws a straight punch, or if you end up *Crashing* into his arms, use the same arm as the arm you have *Crashed* into to pull him into the *Arm Control*.

- If your opponent throws a straight right and you *Crash* into his right arm, use your right arm/hand to yank his wrist and your left arm/hand to grab behind his elbow.

- If your opponent throws a straight left and you *Crash* into his left arm, use your left arm/hand to yank his wrist and your right arm/hand to grab behind his elbow.

Notice how gray shirt has used his right hand to grab at blue shirt's wrist and his left hand to grab behind blue shirt's elbow.

7.2.4 The Crack

Blue shirt uses the "Crack" against gray shirt's left hook. He follows up with a left knee strike.

The *Crack* isn't part of the *Fundamental Five*, but it is something you should be comfortable with. It is half way between a *Crash* and a hack...a cra-ck. And, it fits in the "crack" between an opponent's punching arm and his neck. I prefer the *Smack And Hack* as a default attack entry, and I prefer the *Crash* as a default response against punching attacks. Despite that, sometimes the *Crack* happens, particularly when you're about to attack an opponent with the *Smack And Hack*, but he launches a punch right before you begin. One arm hacks the opponent's neck as the other wedges inside of his punching arm as a shield.

If you're training so that your partner always attacks and you always *Crash* in response, then the *Crack* won't come out naturally. And if you're only training attacking your partner with the *Smack And Hack* or *Palm Blast* entry, you also won't find a use for the *Crack*. However, you will likely find that it occurs out in the context of scenario training, where you don't know if your opponent will attack you first, or if you need to attack him first. (For scenario training, see the next chapter.) While it may not be the ideal defense, you should be comfortable with follow ups from the *Crack* position in case you end up there.

200

Gray shirt attacks blue shirt with a right hook. Blue shirt uses the Crack to defend and yanks gray shirt into a knee, followed by an elbow.

If your hands are in a "back off position", as in the first picture in the series above, with your hands on an imaginary center line between you and your opponent, both hooks and straight punches will come in on the outside of your hands/arms. This makes it relatively easy to simply open your arms and dive in toward your opponent, covered against any strike and getting to the *Crack* position. On the following page, the *Crack* is demonstrated against a straight right cross.

Blue shirt demonstrates the use of the Crack against gray shirt, who attacks with a straight right punch. In the second image you can see the gray shirt's punch will come in on the outside of blue shirt's left hand. This allows blue shirt to easily wedge his arm in as a shield against the punch. In the fourth image, you can see that gray shirt cannot strike blue shirt with his left hand due to the pressure blue shirt can put on gray shirt's neck with the "hacking" arm.

7.2.5 Takedown Defense

Gray shirt attempts to rush in and tackle blue shirt as a counter to blue shirt's attack. Blue shirt uses the "Takedown Defense" as a default response, stopping gray shirt's entry. Blue shirt follows with a hook to gray shirt's jaw.

The FSD *Takedown Defense* is a default response that works extremely well against tackles, single and double leg takedowns, and even high line grappling/wrestling attempts such as bear hugs. It blocks your opponent's entry by putting the bone in your upper arm between the two of you, perpendicular to your opponent, relying on structure rather than muscular strength. With practice, a small woman can use this defense against a much larger and stronger man with relatively little difficulty. Unlike many takedown defenses taught in MMA and wrestling, the FSD *Takedown Defense* allows you to continue standing.

The mechanics of the defense are simple. When your opponent enters, you drop your elbow on the side he is entering on and extend your shoulder forward. If he enters on the side where your leg is back, you leave that leg back. If he enters on the side where your leg is forward, you bring your forward leg back to the rear. Your arm that is not directly stopping the entry goes down in a sweeping motion to block your opponent's arm.

The *Takedown Defense* will end in a position similar to the *Head And Arm Control*, and you can use most of the *Head And Arm Control* follow up techniques from it. See the following pages for additional examples.

Gray shirt attempts to tackle blue shirt with a single leg takedown. Blue shirt blocks the attack with the Takedown Defense. Notice that because gray shirt enters on blue shirt's lead side, blue shirt must step back with his rear leg. This puts his leg beyond gray shirt's reach and solidifies blue shirt's structure. Blue shirt throws gray shirt off to his side after stopping the attack.

Practice maintaining the *Takedown Defense* position against an opponent who is trying to tackle you or put you in a bear hug. It's important to stay as relaxed as possible and let your bone structure do the work. If your opponent drops, you should lower and sink your elbow, but still maintain the perpendicular upper arm position relative to your opponent. In the context of stand up grappling, your opponent may attempt to quickly "pop" your elbow up with his hand, in order to drop under it and grab you. Practice allowing him to do this, and notice how easy it is to maintain your elbow position despite his attempts.

The key to doing the *Takedown Defense* properly is to maintain the solid structure with a relaxed and adaptable flexibility, moving with your opponent rather than against him if he tries to get around or break through your defense. Practice the *Takedown Defense* against simple tackle attacks, and also against takedown attempts during your own attacks. It is crucial that you're able to quickly move from *Blasting* to the *Takedown Defense*, as this is one of the most likely times an opponent will attempt to take you down, in order to avoid your strikes.

Gray shirt attempts to grab blue shirt's lead leg. Blue shirt uses the Takedown Defense to stop him. In the third image blue shirt has gray shirt in a modified "Head And Arm Control" and can finish with any of the follow ups demonstrated at the beginning of this chapter.

7.2.6 Clinch Entry

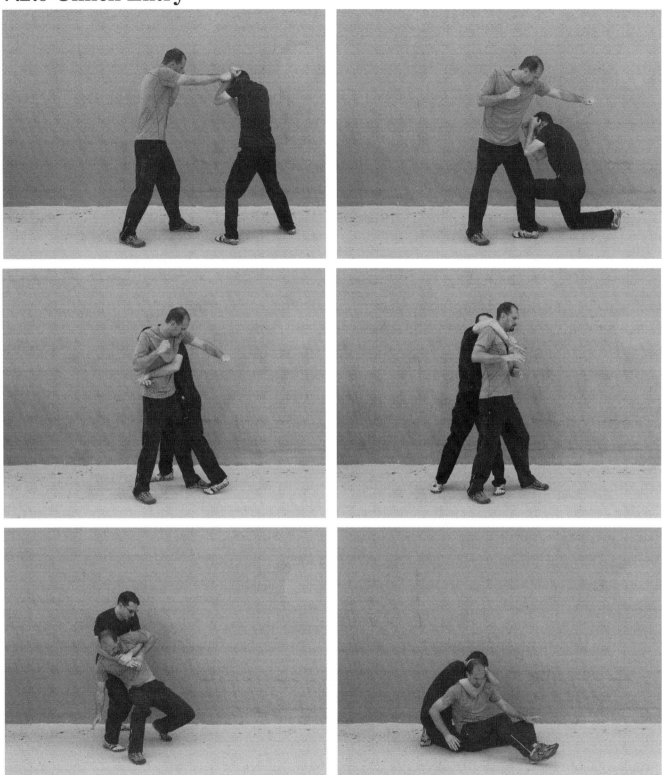

Blue shirt is getting pummelled and overwhelmed by gray shirt, so he drops and enters to the clinch in order to change the game and turn the tables. Blue shirt lunges forward while keeping his head covered, and then steps forward as he rises up, grabbing gray shirt in a "bear hug" or body lock. He then secures the "harness" and brings gray shirt down into a rear choke.

The *Clinch Entry* is a last ditch default response to be used when you're getting pummelled or over-whelmed by a striking attack, and when you're not in a position to *Crash*. The aim of the *Clinch Entry* is to change the game. Your opponent sees you standing one second, and the next you have dropped under his striking attack, immediately rising up and forward, putting him in the clinch. Most often you'll find that the *Clinch Entry* puts you fully to the side of your opponent where you can easily take his back.

From the side-rear position you can strike, choke, or throw your opponent. Face grabs and techniques demonstrated at the beginning of this chapter can also work well.

Some practitioners may choose to use the *Clinch Entry* as a default response against any striking attack, in place of the *Crash,* for example. My preference is only to use it as a last resort. I prefer the control positions that come from the *Crash* or *Palm Blast*. Given the chance, I would prefer to *Crash* or to drop and intercept a striking attack with a *Blast* interception of my own, leading to a stronger control position (*Head And Arm* or *Arm Control*) if necessary. Dropping and throwing a low jab or cross to the opponent's solar plexus can have a similar "turn the tables" effect. However, for practitioners who prefer wrestling, the *Clinch Entry* may be used more often.

Take-Aways

- You must go beyond the *MMA Base* for self defense.
- The key to taking out an opponent is gaining control of the opponent.
- Train default responses that quickly give you control of your opponent, and maximize follow up options. These default responses should be trained to the point that they become conditioned reactions to general classes of attacks.
- Your default responses must be trained against an uncooperative partner, and your follow ups will be dictated by his reactions.
- Your *MMA Base* training will prepare you in case your default/conditioned response fails.

Chapter 8
Environmental Applications

Environmental Applications

For most practitioners, physical self defense takes place in martial arts schools, gyms, and rooms designed for training. Not only are these physical environments unnatural, but the situations and scenarios are also artificial. Practitioners generally know when, where, and even how their opponent will attack. Natural environments and real attackers are another world entirely. Chapter 5 covered the physical difference between natural environments and training environments, along with suggestions for where to train to compensate for this difference. In this chapter, I'll address the application of physical self defense strategy and techniques in natural environments.

In physical self defense and martial arts training, one thing you always know is that there will be a physical conflict. You know your opponent will attack you, or that you will attack him. There is no decision to be made regarding whether you should "fight" or not. And even in the vast majority of hard core training, you know you'll generally be safe. You know your opponent isn't literally going to try to kill you. Even in "no holds barred" competitions against an aggressive opponent, you know there are rules, a referee, and people standing by to help if you are injured. This knowledge makes a tremendous difference, and this difference is under-appreciated.

Choices, considerations, and fear will slow you down. They'll cause you to hesitate while you decide what you should do. Is the man walking toward you and asking for directions trying to close the distance in order to attack you, using his question to mask his unusual breach of distance in an isolated place, or is he simply someone who is lost? Is the man asking you for change just an average beggar? Or, is he going to physically attack you? If you're aware and attentive, sometimes it may be obvious. But at other times it won't be. You won't know with certainty if you should attack or not. And in that moment of hesitation, your attacker will have the opportunity to execute his attack. When you don't know what to do, but your opponent does, you will be at a significant and exploitable disadvantage.

I'll relate a story to illustrate this point.

At the college I attended was a martial arts instructor who happened to be from New Orleans, my home town. I had only met him once, but we had a mutual friend who told me about an attack during which he was badly beaten. The instructor had been walking down a street with his girlfriend when three young teenagers approached them. All three were substantially smaller than he was, and he had an expandable baton in his back pocket. I have little doubt that in a competition or in a training gym, this instructor could have annihilated these three boys, especially with his expandable baton. However, in this situation, he didn't know if these boys were going to attack him or not. He was on a pretty crowded street. And, probably rightly so, he didn't instantly pull his baton and start beating them. One second the boys were mouthing off. Should he do something? When? But the next second the instructor was on the ground, getting kicked in his face. Among other injuries, his lip was split completely open, requiring expensive reconstructive surgery.

A 3rd degree black belt, a martial arts instructor with an expandable baton in his pocket, was severely beaten by three skinny kids. In the training room, these kids wouldn't have had a chance. So what happened? It's easy to say that he wasn't attentive or aware enough. And, maybe he didn't have a good enough default response to the surprise punch that knocked him to the ground. But there is more to it.

As humans, we're only able to concentrate on one thing at a time. Try reading and talking about something different, simultaneously. You cannot. You may be able to talk to a training partner during light sparring. But deciding whether to fight or not, while talking, is like trying to read and talk at the same time. It's impossible, and will result in you doing both things poorly. The martial arts instructor in the above example was being engaged in a conversation of sorts. The kids were talking to him, probably asking him a question, and his brain was busy coming up with a response when he got nailed in the face. It's a common tactic used by criminals. They'll ask you a question right before attacking. If you've never experienced it, you'll be surprised at how difficult it is to effectively respond to an attack while your brain automatically considers the question.

Everyone who trains physical self defense needs to train scenarios like this, first to understand the problem, and then to develop a solution.

Exercise: Have a training partner walk up to you from a distance, and ask you a question as he is approaching. Tell him to think of the question before hand, and ask you a different question each time. You have to answer the question. Sometimes he should thank you and move on. Sometimes he should attack you just as you consider or begin answering the question. Sometimes he should slowly invade your space, attempt to shake your hand, or put his arm around you, before either leaving or then attacking. But you won't know what he'll do. If you've never done this before, it will be eye opening.

The combination of having your brain engaged by a question and not knowing what your opponent will do, if you should attack, or if you should defend yourself, will make it very difficult for you to act as you would in training. Surprisingly difficult. It's not enough to read this. You need to experience it. So next time you train, do the above exercise. It's important that you play both sides. You'll not only discover how difficult it is to respond effectively, but also how easy it is when you are in control, to distract an opponent before you take them by surprise. Combine this with social conventions, such as our natural inclination to shake a person's hand when it is offered, not to be "rude", and you've got a level of difficulty and complexity that far exceeds what is typically experienced in the vast majority of martial arts and self defense training.

8.1 Pre-Positioning

I explained a bit about *pre-positioning* in Chapter 3, on awareness and prevention, as it relates to avoiding the freeze response. *Pre-positioning* also applies to physical self defense.

I have a two part rule I give my students: *Maintain a safe distance. If you feel threatened and cannot escape, blast.* It appears to be simple, but it includes everything written in this book. "Maintaining a safe distance" and "feeling threatened" requires awareness and the use of distance and position. "Cannot escape" implies that you have tried to escape. And the "blast" includes a default response that follows the principle of the *Covered Blast*.

Pre-positioning is about both distance and relative position, but even more importantly, it is about the mental switch you must make in order to control distance and position. That mental switch transforms you from a potential victim into a potential attacker. It takes your focus off of whatever question, statement, or distraction your opponent is making, and on to the physical requirements necessary for an attack to take place, an attack that *you* will execute *if necessary*.

When approached by a potential threat, maintain a safe distance. "Safe distance" means as far away as you can possibly get, and as quickly as reasonably possible. At a minimum, it means far away enough so that the threat cannot touch you without stepping forward first. Obviously, you cannot maintain a safe distance against every person, but as explained in Chapter 3, you don't need to. You only need to maintain this distance against potential threats, and Chapter 3 covered identifying threats in great detail.

If you don't identify the threat until it is too close, create distance and/or superior position. Move to the outside of the opponent's reach, to the outside of his front leg, so that you have the option to attack him with both hands from his "blind side". If there are multiple opponents, then move to the outside of the group as you create distance. The combination of safe distance and superior position will allow you to see an attack coming, and to intercept it as it comes in. But equally important, if a threat doesn't allow you to maintain your distance and position, then you know you have a problem.

No well-meaning person is going to continue to invade your space after you have made it obvious, via both words and actions (see Chapter 3 on using the "Back off" command), that you do not want them coming closer. That's worth repeating: *No well meaning person will continue to invade your space once you've made it obvious that you do not want them to.* This is why my simple rule makes sense. If you feel threatened and have tried to escape, but cannot, you have a real problem on your hands. If you cannot escape, then it's time to resort to physical self defense.

It's worth reiterating here that in many cases escaping includes giving an attacker what he wants. If an attacker pulls a gun and tells you to give him your money, then giving him your money is probably your lowest risk option, and your best way to escape. But if your attacker then tells you to come with him, to get in his car, etc., then you cannot escape, and it's time to fight back, to blast until your attacker is no longer a threat.

If you are highly skilled, you may be able to use a physical control to establish or re-establish distance, position, or control, without disabling your opponent. This may be enough to prevent the attack. Otherwise, you'll need to use a default response, to *Hit And Run* or *Blast*. If your opponent attacks before you're able to, you can use the *Crash* against any high line attack, and the *Takedown Defense* against a grabbing/grappling attack. If you're being overwhelmed, the *Clinch Entry* is an option. Sometimes, you'll be about to attack when your opponent attacks, and your response may be a mix of a *Blast* and a *Crash*, as in the *Crack*. Here is an example of the *Crack* occurring in scenario based training:

Continued on next page...

Beginning on the previous page, gray shirt is walking along and notices blue shirt standing in a strange place and doing what could be a "witness check", looking in the opposite direction before moving toward gray shirt. Due to gray shirt's awareness, he attempts to maintain a safe distance against blue shirt, telling blue shirt to "back off". Blue shirt doesn't listen, and continues to move into gray shirt's space. Gray shirt is about to attack blue shirt, but blue shirt throws a punch before he is able to. Gray shirt reflexively blocks as he enters, using the "Crack". He follows with a knee and an elbow, disabling blue shirt.

When you use the type of scenario training demonstrated in the previous images, make sure to include conversation. The "threat" should ask a question, with the "defender" not knowing what the question will be. The threat should continue to attempt to engage the defender even if the question is answered. For example:

Threat: "Hey man, you got the time?"

Defender: "Nope."

Threat: "You don't have a watch or a phone?"

Defender: "Back off!"

Threat: "What's your problem man? Are you afraid of me?"

At any point in this "conversation" the threat can launch his attack, or simply give up and walk away. Well outside of the safe distance range, it will be possible for the defender to answer a question coherently. But as the safe distance line is getting crossed, the defender may find that the only way he can remain prepared is to shift focus to *pre-positioning*, attacking, or defending, without paying attention to the threat's verbal distractions. This phenomenon will be magnified in a real self defense situation.

Most people who have been seriously attacked can relate to the "auditory exclusion" that occurs when your brain acutely focuses on a single threat, ignoring all else. This may also happen when you switch into the *pre-positioning* mode outside of a training scenario.

Tunnel vision is another common problem in self defense situations, where all you see is the single opponent in front of you. When using scenario training such as the drill above, you should add a more difficult version where additional potential threats are present. Have the other threats move around. Sometimes they should simply watch. Other times they can walk away, or they can join in on the attack, grabbing you to help the initial attacker, attacking with strikes or with weapons.

Here is another example of scenario training, where the *Crash* is used:

Blue shirt approaches gray shirt in a threatening manner. Gray shirt attempts to maintain distance, but blue shirt quickly attacks. Gray shirt crashes, and yanks blue shirt into an elbow.

8.2 Using Your Environment

Another valuable training exercise is to use objects in your environment against your opponent, and when you're on the other side, to avoid having them used against you. Unless you're in an open field, there will be a variety of objects in your environment, from solid walls, corners, and cars to planters and garbage cans. One drill I like to do is to end each defense by slamming my opponent into something or over something. Use the *Head And Arm Control*, *Arm Control*, or a face grab, and slam your opponent's head into a wall, corner, or object. Shove your opponent over an object, causing him to fall.

Throwing objects at your opponent can also work extremely well. Mud, rocks, a handful of coins, or even keys, thrown hard at your opponent's face, can create a great opening for you to escape or *Blast*.

Keep in mind however that this can be taken too far. Some martial arts and self defense instructors teach practitioners to use everything from rolled up magazines to scarves. *Just because you can use something doesn't mean it's the most effective thing to do!* So after you train to use objects in your environment, take time to think about what you did, and talk to your training partners about it. Figure out what works *and* what doesn't work.

Take-Aways

- The complexities in a natural environment make self defense substantially different from most martial arts and self defense training.
- Design some of your training to mirror natural environments as closely as possible, from the training location to the clothing and pre-fight situations.
- Train to use objects in your environment to your advantage, and to avoid having them used against you.

Chapter 9
Physical And Mental Fitness

Physical And Mental Fitness

Which self defense techniques are good for people who are in bad shape? This is a question I get asked on a regular basis. Unfortunately for people who are in bad shape, there is no easy answer. Aside from the fact that there are no magic techniques, physical self defense requires comprehensive training, strategy, *and* functional techniques, so the odds of successful physical self defense for a person who is out of shape are low. Physical self defense is hard. In addition to the normal stress that full force exertion produces, a self defense situation will raise your heart rate and increase your breathing. A real self defense situation will be like an all out sprint. If you can't sprint, you're going to have serious trouble with physical self defense.

Mental health is also more important than many people realize, particularly for prevention (non-physical defense). In order to prevent an attack, you need to be aware, and nothing will disturb your awareness more than a troubled mind.

Fortunately for most people, getting in good shape, physically and mentally, is not beyond reach. The path is simple. The hard part is staying on the path. But once you get accustomed to being on it, you'll likely want to stay there. In addition to teaching self defense, I was a personal fitness trainer for a number of years. Below are my recommendations for staying fit both for health and to maximize your skill in self defense.

9.1 Exercise

Humans have evolved to be active. We did not evolve to sit in a chair all day, and stare at a screen, Doing so will have a negative impact on our lives. Our bodies are amazing machines that respond to our lifestyles. When we're active, our bodies respond by becoming better at being active. When we use our muscles, we build muscle, become stronger, and increase our ability to use our muscles effectively. When we engage in activities that require endurance, our endurance increases. But the opposite is also true. If you don't use it, you will lose it, guaranteed. Muscle mass requires increased energy consumption even at rest, and our bodies are excellent at maintaining and growing what is necessary (based on lifestyle) and removing what is not, in order to minimize energy costs. Therefore, if you are not active, your body will continuously decrease your ability to be active. But if you are active, your body will continuously increase your ability to be active. To get and stay in shape, you must exercise. For the rest of your life. Self defense training itself is great exercise, as long as you are pushing yourself against fully resisting, uncooperative opponents. But additional training will be beneficial. You should be exercising a minimum of 3 times a week, and a combination of aerobic and strength training is necessary.

For aerobic training, nearly anything will do. Biking, swimming, jogging, hiking, hitting a heavy bag, shadow boxing, and/or your regular self defense/martial arts training, assuming it is physically taxing. A good benchmark in terms of your level of exertion for endurance training is that you should be able to talk, but not easily, due to being "out of breath". It's beneficial to change the intensity of your endurance exercise throughout each session. For example, if you're jogging, jog for 5 minutes, sprint for 30 seconds, walk for a minute, go back to jogging, run as fast as you can for one minute, and repeat. Continuously changing the intensity of your training will maximize the benefits.

For strength training, I highly recommend a combination of weight lifting and exercises that use your body weight. At the foundation of your strength training should be three major exercises: dead lifts, squats, and barbell bench presses. These are the three lifts used in power lifting, and they are outstanding for a variety of reasons. These three exercises require you to use large muscle groups, and they can be done with much heavier weights than exercises that target smaller muscles or muscle groups. Therefore, they'll do more to increase your core strength and bone density than most other exercises. While muscular strength is only one component of a self defense or martial arts technique, it certainly helps to maximize your strength. It will also help you to avoid injuries. For these primary lifts, I would recommend warming up first with light aerobic activity, and then doing 5 or 6 sets, where the first set is a warm up set with 10 or 15 repetitions, dropping down to 8 reps, 6 reps, 4 reps, 2 reps, and then a final "cool down" set. With additional exercises like shoulder presses, tricep extensions, or curls, I would recommend something like 3 sets of 8-10 reps.

I like to break my weight training down into "pushing days" and "pulling days". On a pushing day I do exercises that involve pushing motions (bench press, shoulder presses, tricep extensions, dips, squats, lunges, etc.). On a pulling day I do exercises that involve pulling motions (dead lifts, pull ups, pull downs, curls, etc.). This is a nice way of breaking down your weight training so you work everything in two days, but not on consecutive days. My preference is to alternate weight lifting and aerobic workouts. Of course, there are many other possibilities.

In addition to exercises with traditional weights, I highly recommend the use of TRX straps, kettle bells, and BOSU balls. I travel a lot, often for a month or more at a time, and I take my TRX straps with me on longer trips. If a hotel doesn't have a gym, then I can use my TRX straps in the hotel room. The older you get, the quicker you'll lose your strength and endurance. So it's important to keep up your training if you want to stay healthy and in good shape.

To counteract the negative effects of our modern lives, do whatever you can to avoid too much sitting. For example, if you spend a lot of time in front of a computer, use a set-up that allows you to work standing. If you work at home, you can even consider a "tread mill desk" to walk during some of your work hours.

9.2 Diet

Humans have evolved in environments where sugar was hard to find, and nearly never in refined and concentrated forms, or without fiber to slow its digestion. Eating a healthy diet is easy, and there is no need for any of the diets-of-the-day (Atkins, Mediterranean, Paleo, etc.), which are generally counterproductive in the long run. All you need to do is:

- Avoid processed foods and drinks as much as possible, if not completely.
- Avoid sugar as much as possible.
- Eat plenty of fruits and vegetables.
- Eat lots of whole grain fiber.
- Minimize red/fatty meats.

Basically, eat a balanced variety of whole, natural foods. Keep in mind that fruit juice counts as a processed drink. Because the fiber has been removed, it ends up being not much better than drinking a soda, which you should avoid 100%. Sports drinks are generally just as bad.

9.3 Meditation

For those who have practiced meditation for a significant period of time, it should be no surprise that it has been a part of many martial arts in one form or another. Meditation is an excellent practice for mental health, awareness, and to increase performance in everything you do. For the best results, meditation should not be tied to any religion or dogma, which would be useless at best, and most likely get in the way if not worse.

In theory, meditation is simple. Find a comfortable and quiet place to sit, breath naturally but deeply, and empty your mind. But in practice, this is a lot harder than it sounds. Most people give up well before they're able to achieve significant results. By default, our minds seem to be preoccupied with a continuous stream of thought and chatter, which is not easy to silence. Most people experience "thinking about not thinking" when they first try it, and very few people are able to silence their mind for more than a couple of seconds in the first few hours (if not months) of practice.

Why is it useful to silence the chatter? Generally, the chatter isn't something we consciously control. It can easily get in the way of any particular task we're trying to focus on, distracting us and minimizing our ability to perform at an optimal level. Having a calm and clear mind is the key to high level performance in any activity. And in self defense, awareness is crucial, and nothing kills awareness like a runaway mind, preoccupied with useless chatter.

Even more important for most of us, especially with our modern lives, the chatter can lead to stress. People often wake up with their minds already running, continuously going over things that need to be done and problems that need to be taken care of. Usually, this chatter is not only unproductive, but actually counterproductive. It gets in the way of actually getting things done in the most clear, efficient, and effective manner.

Clearing your mind through meditation is like pushing the reset button. The more you practice it, the longer your mind will remain clear, even after you finish meditating. It will reduce the chatter, leaving you less stressed and better able to accomplish any task.

My preference is to meditate shortly after waking up, for a great start to the day. It's important to find a comfortable place to sit, where you can sit with your back straight. Otherwise, your mind will become preoccupied with your body being uncomfortable, or you'll get tired. I like to use two staggered cushions stacked on top of each other. I sit on the top cushion, "Indian style", and rest my ankles on the second cushion that extends just a bit in front of the one on top. I rest my hands, palms up, inside of each other. Most people meditate with their eyes closed, but my preference is to keep my eyes open and focus my vision on something 10 or 15 feet in front of me, which I feel makes it easier to maintain the same calm and relaxed state outside of meditation.

The easiest way to meditate is to feel or focus on your breathing. Feel your breath coming in and out, slowly and deeply. Be in the NOW. Silence your mind by not thinking about the past or the future. Just exist in the moment. It is easier said than done, but with practice, you can do it. If a thought arises (and they will), something in your environment moves, or if you hear a noise, notice and accept it, but don't stick to it. Remain in the present in the now.

In my experience and in the experience of many others, this practice will not only reduce stress and increase performance, but it will also lead to deep realizations that few people arrive at. Being in the moment, you will realize how unimportant and temporary many of your concerns or thoughts are. You'll realize that you can solve any problems you may have, and that you really don't need to be stressed about them. You're ok right now. And the fact of the matter is, it takes very little to be ok. Being in the now, the past won't have the same grip on you that it has on most people. In the now, you can go in any direction you want. The path of your past does not dictate the path of your future. At any point in the future, you can choose to do whatever you want. Your options and choices, your freedom, will expand, because illusionary mental boundaries and limitations will disappear.

You'll find that after you mediate, you notice much more in your environment. You may take a walk, even just walking to your car to go to work, and notice how the wind is blowing leaves around. Or you may notice birds flying and singing. With less chatter and more awareness, you will see more. This has great self defense ramifications, but even greater ramifications for your life. You'll appreciate good food even more, and bad food even less. You'll appreciate good friends and family more, and pay them better attention. You will be more present.

After meditating, my preference is to slowly get up, look outside for a little while, make myself a glass of tea, and sit quietly, enjoying it. During this quiet time, I decide what I want to do during the day, in a calm, clear, and relaxed way. Then, I go about doing it.

If you have negative issues in your life, meditation will bring them out. When the chatter goes away, what comes back first is typically what is really important in your life. For some people, this is reason to stop meditating, going back to a life of stress and dissatisfaction, rather than addressing the negative causes. But for those who persevere, a path can be set upon to remove the causes of negativity, leading to a happy and fulfilling life, with less chatter and a great deal of enjoyment. I highly recommend it.

Chapter 10
Frequently Asked Questions

Frequently Asked Questions

I receive questions from visitors to my website on a daily basis, and in this chapter I'll answer a few of the questions that people most frequently ask, particularly those that may not have been directly answered earlier in this book.

What should I do if I don't have a training partner?

If you don't have a training partner, the first thing you should do is find one. You can learn most skills necessary for awareness and prevention without a partner, but you cannot learn physical self defense without a partner.

Every physical self defense situation involves an attack of some sort, and you cannot learn how to defend against an attack without the existence of the simulated attack. Trying to learn physical self defense without a partner would be like trying to learn to play the guitar without a guitar, or learning to swim without water. It is not possible.

Training on a heavy bag or a dummy is great (and recommended) for exercise, repetition, and developing power. But your training gear doesn't threaten you, move, attack, or counter attack. A real opponent will be fully resisting and uncooperative. In order to learn how to deal with those aspects, you must practice actually dealing with them.

Trying moves on your wife, children, brother, sister, or friend doesn't count. You need a serious training partner or school where you can get serious, regular practice for a long period of time. You and your partner must be willing to work hard, to strike, grapple, get hit, and be uncomfortable. Friends and family members who aren't interested in serious training are not going to provide enough realistic force and resistance, and you won't be able to apply your techniques with realistic force on them, either.

How can I train alone?

You can practice any footwork and/or striking techniques alone. You can practice them in the air, on a heavy bag, or on a dummy. You can use the combinations shown in this book, make up combinations on your own, and practice flowing from technique to technique, imagining a real opponent or opponents in front of you.

Keep in mind however, that solo training should be reserved only for when you do not have a partner available, and most of your training should be with a partner. It is not possible to practice clinch or ground grappling alone.

What is the best self defense I can learn if I don't have much time for training?

Awareness and prevention. The vast majority of attacks can be prevented without resorting to physical self defense.

Physical self defense is complex and multidimensional. In a physical self defense situation, two people will be trying their hardest to injure each other, doing everything they can to stop their opponent from doing what he or she wants. It is alive, and constantly changing. In the space of a second or two, a physical self defense situation can go from stand-up striking to the clinch to ground grappling with a great deal of speed, force, and chaos.

Some instructors teach "weekend self defense courses", and claim that attendants can learn to defend themselves in a couple of days. While it might be possible for an exceptionally talented person with a photographic memory to intellectually understand a handful of techniques or a given curriculum, techniques alone are not enough. The only way to learn to apply techniques in the chaos of a real self defense situation is with serious and continuous training. It takes time and repetition to ingrain techniques so that they can be instinctively used under pressure.

It's certainly possible to get lucky using a technique that you learned and never really trained, and any form of physical resistance in certain situations can be better than none. But to really learn physical self defense, you will need to devote a significant amount of time to training. Twice a week for an hour or two each session is a good minimum, and at that level of commitment, for someone who has never trained self defense or martial arts, it will likely take months before you begin to develop functional skills you can use.

If you don't have enough time to train, I recommend primarily focusing on awareness and prevention, and considering carrying a weapon, such as pepper spray. But, you will also need to train to use the pepper spray, simple as it may seem. It must be in your hand, you'll still need to see the attack coming, and you'll still need to be able to control distance and position via footwork. My next book will cover weapon use and defense in detail.

What is the best self defense for women?

In terms of physical self defense, there is no significant difference between what a woman and a man should learn. All physical attacks involve a combination of striking and wrestling. Strikes are strikes, and wrestling is wrestling. The motivation for an attack against a man and a woman may be different in some situations, but the physical aspects of the attacks will be largely the same. A woman *might* be more likely to initially face "wrestling" as a man attempts to control her. And, a man *might* be more likely to initially face striking. But either can happen to men or women, and the nature of striking, wrestling, and defending against both is always the same.

On average women are smaller and weaker than men. But there are no magic techniques that will work better for a woman than for a man. In the vast majority of situations, if an eye jab, knee to the groin, or choke is the best technique for a man, it is also the best technique for a woman.

Women may face different approaches, as the attacker closes the distance. For example, a man may be more likely to approach a woman offering to help carry groceries. Women may also have different social conditioning in terms of the perception of what is rude and not. But the same principles apply in awareness and prevention for both men and women. Every individual must consider how these principles apply to themselves.

Therefore, there is no such thing as a "best self defense system" for women, or a "best self defense course" for women. What works is what works. In addition, it would be ideal for women to train in a class that includes both men and women. Training in a women-only environment is less realistic in terms of the type of attacker a woman may face.

I have young children. What is the best form of self defense for them?

Again, awareness and prevention. It is unrealistic to think that a small child will be able to physically defend against an adult. I recommend that all parents read the book *Protecting the Gift*, by Gavin De Becker, an outstanding book on how to keep children safe.

In terms of physical practice, my opinion is that practicing systems like judo, Brazilian jiu jitsu, or wrestling is ideal for children. Training in such systems will get kids comfortable with rough physical situations, increase their confidence, and develop their ability to deal with a fully resisting, uncooperative opponent. While MMA, boxing, or Thai boxing are functional systems and great exercise for kids, my concern with those styles is that punching and kicking other kids may lead to an unhealthy type of competitive aggression, particularly for very young children. So my preference is to start younger children with wrestling based styles and move to striking in the early teen years.

How long will it take me to learn self defense?

This is an impossible question, which leads to many more questions. How often will you practice? How fast do you learn? How coordinated are you? What is "learning self defense" to you? Does it mean defending against a single unarmed individual who is the same size as you? Against two men, both larger and stronger than you? Against a gun threat? A knife attack?

Learning physical self defense requires hard work, time, and dedication. Unfortunately, there are no short cuts. If there were, then they would be quickly negated, as any decent attacker would also learn them, and you'd be back on equal footing.

You can learn to be aware of your surroundings and to prevent the vast majority of attacks by reading the chapter in this book on awareness and prevention, carefully considering it, and putting it into practice in your life. You can realistically do that in a day or two, and stop 99% of attacks. But physical self defense is a long term commitment that never ends. Fortunately, it's outstanding exercise and a great deal of fun. So if you're inclined to begin training, I highly recommend it not only for the self defense benefits, but also for fun.

I want to learn self defense that doesn't hurt or injure my opponent. What is the best system or technique for that?

All physical self defense requires defense against striking, grappling, and potentially weapons. No matter how you'd like to stop an attacker, you must absolutely be able to defend against those things. And the only way to learn to defend against something is to train using and defending against it. Therefore, the first step in any physical self defense practice is to develop a functional, strong base in striking, wrestling, and the use of and defense against weapons.

Self defense systems that only train defensive techniques, passive techniques, or techniques that supposedly avoid injuring an opponent will not work in reality, as the training will not sufficiently prepare practitioners for the nature of a real attack.

No matter what type or style of self defense a person wants to learn, I highly recommend training the techniques of the *MMA Base*, as covered in this book. The *MMA Base* gives practitioners the ability to strike and defend against strikes, and to wrestle and defend against wrestling. Once a practitioner has functional skills in the *MMA Base*, then it will be possible to apply techniques that cause no or minimal injury to their training partner. These techniques will primarily consist of "wrestling" or "grappling". Joint manipulations or locks can be used, but only to the point of subduing an opponent. Joint manipulations that progress to breaking the joint will cause more damage than most striking attacks, and this will typically be serious, life-long damage.

The techniques and training methods in this book can be used to defend yourself without injuring your opponent by gaining control and then putting your opponent on the ground or in a hold from which he cannot escape or do damage to you (see Chapter 7). You can also use the *Arm Control* or *Head And Arm Control* as "holds", keeping in mind that your opponent will be able to move to some degree, and you'll need to adapt to his movements.

How can I defend against a bigger, stronger, or faster opponent?

Defending against someone who is larger, stronger, and/or faster than you is going to be harder than defending against someone who matches you physically. But the principles of defense are going to be the same, and you should use the *Covered Blast* (Chapter 4) no matter the attacker's size.

Against a smaller or weaker opponent, you may be able to easily palm blast right through them. Against a larger/stronger opponent, taking a more angular/indirect approach may be more effective. You might start with a *Hit And Run* approach, trying to nail your opponent while staying out of his way. But consider that if you need to stay in the game and the *Hit And Run* doesn't take your opponent out, you'll have to enter again.

Control is the key to physically dominating any opponent, and because control positions like the *Arm Control* and *Head And Arm Control* will keep you safe while giving you the opportunity to repeatedly attack your opponent, they make ideal positions to use on larger, stronger, and faster opponents. These positions will minimize your opponent's ability to effectively use his physical advantages.

Against a smaller opponent, you may easily succeed using less damaging techniques (palm strikes, low kicks, and throws for example). Against a larger, more dangerous opponent, escalating the severity of your techniques may be necessary. Eye strikes, knees to the groin, elbows to the head, hacks to the neck, chokes, and head manipulations may be necessary. Unlike many punching and wrestling techniques, these damaging techniques work equally well and are equally damaging on opponents of any size.

Although defending against a larger opponent is more difficult, by using the principles of the *Covered Blast*, the control positions covered in this book, angular footwork, and your most damaging techniques, you should be able to turn the odds in your favor, successfully taking out opponents much larger, stronger, and faster than you.

Although weapon use is not covered in this book, weapons will dramatically increase your ability in self defense. My next book will cover weapon use and defense in depth.

What can I do to improve my footwork?

Footwork provides the foundation for all techniques, and in many martial arts and self defense systems, footwork training is seriously lacking. Every technique you perform should have an element of footwork. When you strike, you should always train moving forward, sideways, at an angle, and even backwards. Remember that when you strike or attempt to strike an opponent, he will move! He will either move because you hit him, or he will move to avoid your attack. So whenever you practice techniques, make sure to practice them with different types of footwork.

The basic *Cross* and *Triangular* footwork demonstrated in Chapter 6 of this book is the foundation for all footwork. You can train this footwork alone or with a partner. Think of different patterns that you can drill, repeat, and change.

Angular footwork is often the most effective for self defense, allowing you to move to places where your opponent cannot attack you, but where you can attack him. It also provides cover and safety when launching an attack of your own. Pay close attention to the footwork used throughout this book, particularly in Chapter 7, and make it a part of your training. In short, the answer is, practice. Make footwork a part of everything you do.

What do you think about (insert specific martial art)?

When I consider the value of a particular martial art, I look at the strategy, techniques, training methods, and the range it covers. For a martial art to be complete as a self defense system, it must have a sound strategy, functional techniques, functional training methods, and it must cover all ranges (stand-up, clinch, and ground), with and without weapons. It is *exceedingly rare* for a single martial art to cover all of this, which is why I created the FSD system.

The same martial art may also be taught differently depending on the teacher. Japanese ju jutsu for example is a relatively complete system, encompassing stand-up, clinch, and ground, striking and grappling. Some Japanese ju jutsu teachers may teach weapon use and defense, and some may not. But more importantly, some may use functional training methods, and others may not.

On the other hand, most martial art styles do not come close to encompassing the full range of techniques and situations, no matter who the teacher is. Aikido does not include strikes. Brazilian jiu jitsu does not include strikes. Boxing does not include grappling. Most karate styles do not include grappling. With technically limited styles, no matter how good the teacher is, or how good the training is, the style will be incomplete as a comprehensive self defense system.

But just because a specific martial art is incomplete, does not make it bad or ineffective. However, most martial arts will need to be combined with other systems in order to be complete. For the *MMA Base*, you'll need to train a variety of techniques from boxing, Thai boxing, wrestling, and Brazilian jiu jitsu. For more functional self defense techniques you may draw from the *MMA Base* systems and others... wing chun, Japanese jiu jitsu, Chinese chi na, various Filipino martial arts, and so on.

So when considering the value of a particular system as it relates to learning self defense, you should look for how complete the system is, what you may or may not need to add, and what you will or won't get from the training methods. There may be a number of good techniques in Shotokan Karate for example, but the training (almost all solo or prearranged) is typically so ineffective that it would likely be a waste of time to study for self defense. The techniques of boxing may not be optimal for self defense, primarily due to close fisted punching, but the training is so good (primarily against an uncooperative opponent), and the technique so easily adapted for use in self defense, that it is worth training.

With the exception of ground fighting, the techniques and training methods in this book are comprehensive for unarmed self defense. If you have a serious and committed training partner, follow them, and add a ground fighting system such as Brazilian jiu jitsu.

If you are currently training in a particular martial art, or considering doing so, then I recommend thinking in the terms I mentioned above, using the knowledge you have gained in this book regarding functional techniques, training methods, and strategy. Add techniques and training methods that are missing, and focus on the most functional and effective techniques and training methods in the material you're practicing.

What are your thoughts on Krav Maga?

I'll specifically address Krav Maga here, since I tend to get so many questions regarding it. I consider Krav Maga to be one of the most effective, widely available systems today. If you're looking for a martial arts school and your primary goal is physical self defense ability, Krav Maga is likely to be the best option.

With that said, the quality of the material and instruction, as always, depends on the teacher. For example, in my experience, many Krav Maga teachers train students to punch with a closed fist. I think this is a mistake, as the chance of breaking your hand if you punch someone hard, in the head, and without a glove, is relatively high.

I'm also not crazy about many of the stick, knife, and gun defenses commonly taught in KM. I do think they're far better than the vast majority of what you'll find in traditional martial arts, and they can certainly work. But I think there are better alternatives in many cases.

Despite the relatively minor issues I have with some KM techniques, the system is 100% self defense focused, and the training tends to be very good and functional. So while I prefer the particular techniques covered in this book, and the weapon use and defense that will be covered in the next FSD book, if you're looking for a self defense school to train at, KM may be your best widely available option.

Can you recommend a martial art for me to take?

See the answers to the previous two questions.

I recommend training the material in this book with a serious partner or partners. But if you don't have a training partner and are looking for a self defense school, I would consider Krav Maga, an MMA school, or a combination of martial arts that gives you comprehensive coverage.

The most important thing to have when looking at any martial art is a sceptical mind. Most martial arts are not suited for self defense, but most martial arts instructors will tell you that they are. Consider the material in this book, what makes functional techniques and training methods, and what doesn't. Watch a class or two, talk to the instructor and ask him or her any questions you may have. Above all, always question whatever it is that you're doing, and make sure you can make it work against a completely uncooperative, fully resisting opponent.

What can I do to become more comfortable with sparring or fighting? What can I do to become more confident in my self defense ability?

The best way to get more comfortable with sparring/fighting is to do it more often. The key is to use a smart and gradual progression in both intensity and technical scope. As outlined in this book, sparring shouldn't be dangerous or scary. As long as you begin with the appropriate light intensity and limited techniques, and progress as you feel comfortable, you will get to the point where you are comfortable and confident in your ability.

The problem with most sparring I've seen in traditional martial art schools is that there is very little guidance or progression. Students train techniques alone and in short, prearranged drills, and are then told to "go spar". They end up learning nothing, often getting hurt, and the "techniques" they use in sparring look nothing like the techniques they practice in the rest of their training. If you're attending such a school, you should probably quit! It's no wonder if you're feeling uncomfortable with sparring/fighting.

If you're sparring with the right kind of progression, you may feel a little uncomfortable, but you should never feel afraid. Feeling afraid is a sign that you are sparring at a level that is above your ability.

Competition is a different matter. If you are competing, you may feel anxiety or fear, but this is typically a result of the competition and not so much due to fear of injury or uncertainty regarding what you are doing.

Confidence in self defense ability is similar to with sparring/fighting. The more you train, and the more realistic your training is, the more confident you will become. However, realistic training will also teach you how uncertain the outcome of a self defense situation may be, particularly if you're doing environmental and scenario training, with and without weapons, and with multiple opponents. Realistic, functional training will build confidence, but also the desire to avoid having to use it!

How safe is getting punched in the head during training? Do I need to get punched in the face to learn how to "take a punch"?

Getting hit in the head is not good for your health. A very hard hit can instantly do serious damage to your brain. Even light and moderate hits can cause small injuries that add up over time. The goal of self defense training is to learn how *not* to get hit, rather than how to "take a punch". As explained throughout this book, training can and should be done safely and progressively. At first, your training partner can attack with low intensity and pull his punches if your defense fails. As you get better and better, your training partner can increase the intensity, while still being careful enough not to seriously injure you should your defense fail.

If you are training realistically, you will get hit from time to time. You'll become comfortable with hard physical contact, and will learn to take a punch to the extent that you should. But no one should purposely get hit square in the nose, right on the jaw, or in the head. With proper training and form, if you do get hit, it will likely be a glancing blow and/or a hit to the upper part of your head. You'll be moving, and will likely avoid having your head violently snapped back. Your partner should be good enough and considerate enough to avoid injuring you on a regular basis.

Do you recommend carrying a weapon, and if so which weapon?

This is a complex question, and one that leads to numerous additional questions. First, I only recommend carrying a weapon if you know what it can and cannot do, when to use it, and how to use it.

Second, no weapon is ideal in every situation. A gun may work against an opponent who approaches a woman in an isolated area from a distance, brandishing a knife. But this assumes that the attacker would be stupid enough to show his weapon from a distance, and give his victim enough time to pull her gun. A gun would be a terrible choice in the same situation if there were other innocent people behind the attacker, as they could be killed by stray bullets.

Pepper spray can work in many situations. But it's not a good idea if your attacker is upwind from you on a windy day. Depending on the type of pepper spray you have (the spray profile), it may not be good in a small enclosed area. It certainly isn't good in a close range situation that involves wrestling.

Nevertheless, pepper spray is a good choice for many people. It can work as well or better than many other weapons, in a great variety of situations, and it isn't lethal. The key to using pepper spray is to have it in your hand, and to see the attack coming while you still have time to use it. It's also important to remember that any weapon can fail. It's possible that your pepper spray won't work when you need it to, that you'll miss your opponent, or that it just won't work on him.

In my view, unarmed physical self defense skills should be your base, since you may not have your weapon ready when you're attacked, and you can use them as back up if your weapon fails or if your opponent gets beyond its effective range.

In order for any weapon to work, you must see the attack coming with enough time to access and use your weapon. The use of the weapon needs to be legally justifiable if you don't want to potentially end up jail after the assault. And it needs to actually increase your odds against the threat you are facing. Sometimes a stick or expandable baton is a better choice than a gun. Sometimes a gun is a better choice than a knife.

So the question doesn't have a single easy answer. It depends on who you are, what you can do, what (if any) threats you are likely to face, where, and so on. It requires careful consideration on an individual basis, and training.

What is chi power and how can I learn to use it?

Chi (Chinese) or *ki* (Japanese) is a general term that different people give different meaning to. In my experience, most people who talk about the use of "chi" are talking about magic, which does not exist. Unfortunately, these ideas are often spread by teachers who use tricks and manipulation to mislead students into thinking they are masters of some esoteric and magical art.

A practitioner with a high level of skill can do things that someone with no skill or a low level of skill finds almost unbelievable. This is the same in any art or sport though, not just in martial arts. Because martial arts are physical, the ability to perform high level techniques is often attributed to a certain use of energy, which is called *chi* in Chinese and *ki* in Japanese.

For example, because I have practiced for more than 20 years, I have a corresponding ability to feel where an opponent's energy is coming from, and how to make slight movements or hold positions that neutralize it. I can easily bring beginning students that are twice as big and strong as I am down to the ground with a standing elbow lock. However, the same student cannot get the elbow lock to work on me, despite being much bigger and stronger, and trying with full force. I could pretend that I have a magical ability that will take decades to learn, only through special forms. Or, I can simply explain the mechanics of what I am doing, how I apply force in multiple and changing directions to make my technique hard to resist, and how I prevent my opponent from doing the technique on me by preventing him from getting the angle/leverage he needs to apply the technique. These displays of skill may seem like magic, but there is always a mechanical/scientific explanation. They can be taught without resorting to hocus pocus or mystical woo woo.

Other displays, like shooting "chi balls" from a distance, "no touch knock outs", and levitation, work either by manipulating students into thinking they work, and acting accordingly, or through tricks like those a magician would use. There is no magic!!!

Legitimate use of "energy" or chi in a highly skilled way is nothing more than the expert use of your mind and body. Using the right body mechanics or structure along with exerting your energy in the right places and at the right time, will magnify your ability to apply and resist techniques.

To attain a high level of skill in anything requires exactly the same thing: good training, dedication, and time. If you want to learn how to hit like someone twice your size, how to easily move a much bigger and stronger opponent, or how to resist such techniques working on yourself, the way to do so is straight forward. Practice. With time, your skills will get better and better. You'll develop your "chi", and your ability to use it.

What do you think about using pressure points for self defense?

As with "chi", there is a great deal of hocus pocus surrounding "pressure points". Are there places on the human body that can be pressed or struck to cause damaging results? Yes. But these places are mostly obvious. If you jab your finger into a person's eye or throat, or kick a man between the legs, it's likely to cause damage and have a substantial effect. There are a few additional spots that hurt more than usual when pressed or struck, some of which make good targets and some of which do not. But there is no magic involved.

Pressure points that require multiple penny or dime sized spots to be struck in quick succession in order to work are useless in self defense, especially against an aggressive and uncooperative opponent. Even if they did work, it would be far easier to elbow a man in the jaw or chop him in the neck than it would be to hit three small points on his arm first.

Using pressure or pain points to control or hold an opponent is also unlikely to work against all but the most cooperative partners. Common joint locks and holds that can be found in wrestling or ju jutsu are much more effective.

You claim that (insert martial art) isn't effective for self defense, but how can it not be effective if so many people are practicing it?

People do and believe a great variety of things that are incorrect and even detrimental. Just because a large number of people, even a majority, does something or believes something, that doesn't make it effective, right, or true.

Take religion as an easy example. If you practice a particular religion, no matter what religion it is, most humans on this planet do not share it. Most of them think your religion is wrong, if not extremely silly. And if you consider the details of their religions and/or religious practices, you will likely find them wrong and silly. Yet, that doesn't stop a majority of people from having these beliefs and practices. Most people believe in strange hocus pocus, and many lead their lives and practice accordingly. It doesn't make it right, ideal, true, or effective.

Martial arts and self defense systems are no different. Most people who practice them are never really required to test them. And if they do test them and they fail, they chalk it up to a failure on their part, to not being good enough, or to doing something wrong.

The key to skill in physical self defense is being able to deal with a fully resisting, uncooperative opponent who is trying to take you out by striking and wrestling, with or without weapons. To be able to defend against such an opponent, you must train against a fully resisting, uncooperative opponent. Systems that do that will look remarkably similar. Systems that do not have the potential to take all sorts of differing forms, thus the great variety of ineffective martial arts we see today.

Take Aways

- Self defense and martial arts are two different things.
- Functional self defense requires a comprehensive combination of strategy, techniques, and training methods, including non-physical awareness and prevention.
- Understand what constitutes legal self defense, and be able to communicate how your actions comply with it, or risk prison time and law suits.
- Avoid dangerous places and people. Be a bad target. Be aware of your surroundings, and pay attention to warning signs and pre-attack indicators.
- Maintain a safe distance from potential threats and places they may hide.
- Escape when you feel threatened.
- Give up your money or any other object rather than risking your life, but do not go anywhere with a predator.
- Physical self defense is an absolute last resort, only to be used when your life or the life of someone you care about is in immediate danger and there are no other options.
- Real physical violence is fast, dynamic, chaotic, and dangerous. It is unlike what is trained in most martial art schools.
- Avoiding injury is your first priority in physical self defense, more important than taking out your opponent.
- Use the *Covered Blast* to maximize your options and minimize your risk.
- Every training method has strengths and weaknesses. You must use a combination of methods to make up for the deficiencies inherent in each individual method.
- You must train against opponents who are fully resisting and uncooperative.
- The *MMA Base* is the ideal base from which to learn to strike and defend against striking, and to wrestle and defend against wrestling.
- The key to taking out your opponent without being injured yourself is to get and maintain control of your opponent.
- You should have conditioned *default responses* that work against broad categories of attacks, allowing you to quickly gain control of your opponent even if you are attacked by surprise. The FSD *Fundamental Five* provides exactly that.
- Natural environments are substantially different from most self defense and martial arts training rooms. You must train in natural environments and in realistic scenarios in order to be prepared to defend yourself in them.
- Design some of your training to mirror natural environments as closely as possible, from location to clothing and pre-fight situations.
- Train to use objects in your environment as weapons, and avoid having them used against you.
- Physical and mental fitness is important for self defense. Exercise, eat well, and maintain a clear mind.
- Learn to deal with violence, but don't obsess about it. Life is too short. Focus on the positive, and enjoy yourself!

Made in the USA
Lexington, KY
16 November 2014